THE
BHAGAVAD
GĪTĀ

Translated, with Introduction
and Critical Essays by
Eliot Deutsch

WITHDRAWN

UNIVERSITY
PRESS OF
AMERICA

LANHAM • NEW YORK • LONDON

Copyright © 1968 by

Eliot Deutsch

"Reprinted by arrangement

with Holt, Rinehart and Winston"

University Press of America,™ Inc.

4720 Boston Way
Lanham, MD 20706

3 Henrietta Street
London WC2E 8LU England

Library of Congress Cataloging in Publication Data
Main entry under title:

The Bhagavad Gita.

    Reprint. Originally published: New York : Holt,
Rinehart and Winston, 1968.
    Bibliography: p.
    1. Deutsch, Eliot.
BL1138.G2.E5   1982   294.5'924   81–40512
ISBN 0–8191–1900–8 (pbk.)   AACR2

All University Press of America books are produced on acid-free
paper which exceeds the minimum standards set by the National
Historical Publications and Records Commission.

TO ADLEY

Contents

Preface

To translate the *Bhagavad Gītā* into a Western language is something less than an original undertaking. The *Gītā* has been translated into English, and into most other major European languages, many times by both Western scholars and Indian pandits. It has been commented upon in the Indian tradition repeatedly for over a thousand years and it has been analyzed, criticized, dissected, and sometimes revered, by Westerners for well over a hundred years. However, a text of the poem designed specifically for Western students of philosophy and religion by a Western philosopher or teacher of philosophy is not available; this is the gap which the present work seeks to fill.

Together with the English translation and an Introduction which discusses some of the main concepts employed in the *Gītā* (which are kept in Sanskrit in the Translation), I have included some notes which offer explanations of other Sanskrit terms and a small series of philosophical essays. I would urge that the student consider the essays only subsequent to his confrontation with the text itself and that he be encouraged to work through the text, when possible, in the original language. One's experience with the poem is enriched considerably when one can see how various passages are constructed and how various Sanskrit terms function in different contexts; and, needless to say, the full poetic efficacy of the work can be realized only in the language of its original expression.

In order to appreciate the philosophical-religious significance of the *Bhagavad Gītā*, however, it is not necessary that one read it in Sanskrit. Some linguists, philologists, and other "purists" have overstressed the importance of knowing the original language in which "classics" were written for a comprehension of their philosophical-cultural import. Although something undoubtedly is lost in reading non-English philosophical and religious works only in translation, much can still be gained by a study of these works in English; indeed, for most of us the only real alternative would be not to read them at all.

In my translation I have tried to adhere closely to the original text and at the same time to cast it into a readable English form. I have not, however, deliberately eliminated the apparent inconsistencies and difficulties in the text. Some of these will be dealt with in the essays that follow the translation, and for detailed analyses of the more technical philological and interpretative problems the advanced student is advised to study carefully the classical commentaries by Shankara, Rāmānuja, and Madhva and the comments by distinguished Western scholars such as Franklin Edgerton, Richard Garbe, and W. Douglas P. Hill.

It is always a pleasure to acknowledge one's appreciation to others for their generous assistance and for the time and advice they so graciously give. I am particularly indebted to the American Institute of Indian Studies for making it possible for me to spend a year in India (1963–64), during which time a draft of the translation was made, and to Rensselaer Polytechnic Institute for a research grant which enabled me, after much further labor, to put this draft into a publishable form. I deeply appreciate the help that was given to me by many Indian scholars who embodied so fully the spirit of the *Gītā* in their own lives. I am especially grateful to Dr. G. Palsule of Deccan College, Poona, India, who reviewed and corrected my word-by-word grammatical analysis of the Sanskrit text. Professor Ainslie T. Embree and Professor Arthur Danto of Columbia University read portions of the translation and essays and made many valuable suggestions. My colleague Professor Sterling Olmsted has given me a great deal of encouragement in the writing of this work and has also made a number of helpful suggestions. Professor J. A. B. van Buitenen of the University of Chicago has been generous in sharing his vast knowledge of Indian thought and culture and has raised several questions which proved to be fruitful. I also wish to express my appreciation for the thoughtful responses to my interpretations of the *Gītā* from my students at Rensselaer and at the University of Chicago during the summer of 1966. I have learned more from these students than I like to admit. Lastly I want to express my deep appreciation to my wife for constantly challenging me to clarify obscurities of my own making and for her help in every phase of the work.

The University of Hawaii
Honolulu, Hawaii

July 1967

A Note on the Pronunciation of
Sanskrit Words

Vowels

a – <u>a</u> in America or *o* in come
ā – *a* in far or in father
i – *i* in pit or in pin
ī – *ee* in feel or *i* in machine
u – *u* in put or pull
ū – *u* in rule
ri (r̥) – properly *ur,* but by modern Hindus as *ri* in river or in
　　writ.
e – *ay* in say or *a* in made
ai – *i* in rite or *ai* in aisle
o – *o* in go
au – *ou* in loud

Consonants

Consonants are pronounced approximately as in English, except:
g – *g* in gun or in get　(always "hard")
ch – *ch* in church
sh (ś, ṣ – *sh* in sheet or in shun)
When *h* is combined with another consonant (e.g., *th, bh*), it is
aspirated: *th* as in boa*t*house; *ph* as in u*ph*ill, etc. The palatal
ñ is like the Spanish *señor* (*jña,* however, is pronounced most
often by modern Hindus as "gyah," with a hard *g*).

Accent

The general rule is to accent the next to final syllable, if it is
long, or the nearest long syllable preceding it. If none is long,
the first syllable is accented. (A long syllable is one which con-
tains a long vowel or one in which a vowel is followed by two
or more consonants.)

Introduction to the
GĪTĀ

I

Date and Authorship

The *Bhagavad Gītā* literally means "Song of the Lord," and is, as the title suggests, essentially a religious poem. Although technically it belongs to a class of literature known as *smriti*, "remembered" or "traditional" texts, it has the status in Hindu culture of *shruti*, "scripture" or "revelation." It is in fact the most revered and celebrated text in Hinduism. Countless orthodox Hindus recite passages from it daily, and on special occasions the entire work is recited by groups of devotees. Further, it is taken as one of the three *prasthānas* or "foundations" of Vedānta, which is regarded by most Hindus as the most important tradition of Indian philosophy. The central figures of all the schools of Vedānta, such as Shankara, Rāmānuja, and Madhva, have written commentaries on it.

It is impossible to know precisely when or by whom the poem was composed. It forms only a small part of the great Indian epic, the *Mahābhārata* (Chapters 23 to 40 of the *Bhīshmaparvan*), whose authorship, according to tradition, is that of Vyāsa. But like many other great spiritual works, its author is really anonymous. The *Gītā* was definitely composed later than the (early) *Upanishads* (several passages in it may be found in the *Upanishads* and many of its philosophical concepts are clearly derived from Upanishadic sources) , and earlier than the formulation of the classical philosophical systems in their concise *sūtra* form. This would suggest that the period of the *Gītā's* composition would fall somewhere between the fifth century B.C. and the second century B.C. The final recension of the work was made sometime in the Gupta period (fourth to seventh centuries A.D.) , and the earliest manuscript source dates back to Shankara's commentary in the ninth century.[1] *

Until very recently, Indian scholarship has never been seriously concerned about when or by whom it was written. Westerners are frequently annoyed by the untidy historical consciousness of the Indians, but quite possibly we have much to learn from this disregard for history in matters of the spirit. If there is anything in the poem that is true and valuable, it is true and valuable now and will continue to be so in the foreseeable future.

II

The Philosophical-Religious Position of the Gītā and Explication of Technical Terms Retained in Sanskrit

The main philosophical-religious position of the *Bhagavad Gītā* is that of a "personalized monism" or a "non-dualistic theism." These abstract terms appear, no

* Notes to this Introduction begin on p. 22.

doubt, in their respective conjunction, to be incompatible. A monism which is "personal" ceases, we assume, to be a monism, and a theism, by definition, can never be "non-dualistic." These conjunctions will be critically appraised later on; but one must recognize that the *Gītā* suggests quite explicitly that there is no incompatibility between a non-dualism which upholds the oneness of reality and a theism which sees this oneness as a living spirit.

The *Gītā* is synthetic (if not eclectic) in its philosophical dimensions. It seeks to harmonize many of the trends and ideas in the thought of its time and consequently introduces few new or original technical ideas of its own. It is apparently more concerned to weave what it takes to be meaningful in each divergent philosophical trend into a single whole from its own standpoint of spiritual experience than it is to put forth new philosophical ideas of its own.

To trace all the prior developments in Indian philosophy and religion practice which are presupposed by, or incorporated into, the *Gītā* would require a separate text. It is necessary, though, to understand somewhat the main lines of thought and tradition with which the poem is concerned. In this translation a small number of technical terms have been kept in the original Sanskrit. A firm grasp of these terms will not only avoid the problem of searching for almost always inadequate English equivalents, but it will also give one some hold on these traditional lines of thought which the *Gītā* accepts, develops, and synthesizes.[2]

Following is a brief explication of the technical terms which have been retained in the Sanskrit:

yoga

The term *yoga* is used extensively in the *Gītā* and in a number of different senses. The term is probably derived from the root *yuj*, which means to "yoke" or "harness," and carries the general connotation of "joining" or "uniting oneself with." Following the usage in the *Katha Upanishad* (I, 2, 12), where the expression *adhyātma-yoga* ("yoking with one's real self" or "disciplined meditation on the self") appears, the *Gītā* generally uses *yoga* to mean the controlling of one's lower sensuous nature and the realization of one's higher spiritual nature. It means a *disciplined* detachment from the lower self of desires, of passions, of obsessions, and a realized attachment to that higher self which transcends the will, the emotions, and even the intellect, and which cannot be identified with them.

Yoga is also used as the name for various specific philosophical-religious "disciplines" or "ways" to self-realization. Among the various types of *yogas* distinguished are *karma yoga*, or the "way of action," *bhakti yoga*, or the "path of devotion," and *jñāna yoga*, or the "discipline of knowledge."

The *Gītā* also uses the term *yoga* to denote the system of Indian philosophy which was allegedly founded by Patañjali, a system also known as *rāja yoga*. In it *yoga* is defined as the "cessation of mental modifications" (*citta vritti nirodha*): it is primarily a psychological discipline which also involves various physical postures and breath control and which seeks a state of complete self-integration and freedom. (Most modern writers use the term *yoga* to refer to just this system.)

6

Lastly, *yoga* is sometimes employed in the *Gītā* as a synonym for "divine power." When Krishna, as the Lord, speaks of his *yoga* (as in Chapters X and XI) he does not mean his "way" or "path" but his "creative power."

(Each chapter of the *Gītā* is entitled "The *yoga* of . . . ," but the term is employed here for the most part only in an honorific sense.)

sānkhya; purusha, prakriti

The term *sānkhya* is used in the *Gītā* primarily to mean "mental discrimination" or "intellectual understanding." It is thus at times made synonymous with the word *jñāna* ("knowledge," "spiritual understanding").

Sānkhya, however, is also a name for another of the classical systems of Indian philosophy. The Sānkhya system developed a theory of cosmic evolution or emanation wherein everything in the universe was explained in terms of two basic original principles called *prakriti* ("matter," "unconscious force") and *purusha* ("soul," "spirit," "consciousness"). Through an interaction of these principles, *prakriti* brings forth and constitutes all the things and powers of the world in an ordered succession, and *purusha* is differentiated into a plurality of individual conscious selves.[3]

Now one of the confusing things here is that the *Gītā* will draw heavily upon this system when formulating various conceptual descriptions and schemata. It will make a distinction between *prakriti* and *purusha* and, although it will try to overcome the rigid dualism of Sānkhya, it will follow this system closely in describing

7

the constituents of Nature and the basic categories of existence.

The term *sānkhya*, though, when it appears in the *Gītā*, is not intended to denote the Sānkhya system; rather, it denotes "intellectual understanding," "analytic discrimination," or "knowledge."

dharma

The concept of *dharma*—"duty," "law," "righteousness," "moral merit"—is exceedingly rich in Indian thought in general and in the *Bhagavad Gītā* in particular. The term connotes religious and social duties; that which one ought to perform by virtue of the place which one occupies in the social order, and it further suggests a law of one's own nature (*sva-dharma*), which is understood to be a reflection of one's particular mental-spiritual development. The concept of *dharma* is thus articulated in terms of one's station in life, since this ideally expresses the level of one's development as a spiritual being.

Hindu society is organized traditionally in terms of three interrelated schema: the four *āshramas* or "stages of life," the four *purushārthas* or "aims of life," and the four *varnas*, "social classes" or "castes." According to the first schema, a man's life naturally falls into the various, rather distinct, divisions of youth, maturity, and old age, and one's life ought to be so organized that a fulfillment proper to each stage may be obtained. The term *āshrama* comes from *shram*, "to toil," "to exert oneself," and suggests that there is a special kind of work in the world which corresponds to each of the natural divisions of one's life in the world. The four *āshramas* are (1) the student stage (*brahmacarya*), (2) the householder (*grihastha*), (3) retirement (*vānaprastha*), and (4) renunciation (*sannyāsa*) of the social order. During the student stage, one's *dharma* is to become educated; it is to learn to be a man (in relation to other men and to the Divine), and this means studying the Vedic scripture as well as training one's capacities and talents so that one can function in society with maximum effectiveness. The householder enters into society; he marries, has children, and engages in an occupation which supports his family. When the time comes, however, when he no longer finds satisfaction in this, and when his services are no longer essential to the maintenance of the family, he enters into retirement (*vānaprastha*—literally, a "forest dweller"). He still has the responsibility of offering his guidance in family and community affairs, but he is encouraged to spend his time in study and meditation. Lastly, he is to become a *sannyāsin*—one who renounces the entire social order for the sake of striving for spiritual freedom. The duties enjoined upon him by his previous stages no longer are binding upon him. His only obligation is to seek a self-knowledge and knowledge of reality.[4]

The four aims of life, *purushārthas* (literally, "what is sought by men"), are based upon the recognition that there are different basic drives that condition human experience and which need to be satisfied, redirected, and transcended at appropriate times in one's life. The four aims are (1) *artha* or "wealth," (2) *kāma* or "pleasure," (3) *dharma* or "social duty" (which is related to, but not to be identified with, the general concept of *dharma*) , and (4) *moksha* or "release," "liberation," "freedom." (The traditional ordering of the aims put *dharma* before *artha* and *kāma*; the relations between the aims, however, might best be brought out by treating *dharma* as the third aim.)

Artha is the aim of accumulating and enjoying material things. It is the goal of attaining material necessities and luxuries and of gaining economic and political power. *Kāma* is the aim of having pleasurable experiences such as physical love and aesthetic delight. The term literally means "desire" and, in this context of the *purushārthas*, suggests primarily the aim of satisfying sensual desire. *Artha* and *kāma* are essentially egocentric aims. They pertain to the individual who takes his own needs and desires as the central fact of existence. And hence the necessity for *dharma*, the third aim, which involves an awareness of one's dependence upon others and the consequent recognition that one must adjust one's own needs and desires to those of others; that one must work for the good of all as well as for oneself. *Dharma*, which is to inform the other two aims, represents the aim of one who knows that the individual does not stand alone but is rather a member of a social order which demands that he assume various responsibilities in it. The aim of *moksha* is different in kind from the other three (the *trivarga*, as they are called) . It corresponds precisely to the last stage of life and involves the quest for the realization of a supreme spiritual value to which all other values are subordinated.

The four aims represent a progressive maturing of the self. They are descriptive of the natural growth of a man and, especially with *dharma* and *moksha,* they are prescriptive of the proper development of moral consciousness. As a man passes from studentship to old age, he must transform and transcend just those drives which bind him to his lower nature.

The last of the schema is that of the four *varnas* or "castes." In an ancient hymn of the Rig Veda we read:

> When they divided Purusha [the primal person] how many portions did they make? What do they call his mouth, his arms? What do they call his thighs and feet?

> The Brāhman was his mouth, of both his arms was the Rājanya [Kshatriya] made.
> His thighs became the Vaiṣya, from his feet the ṣūdra was produced.
> [X, 90, 11–12, translated by Ralph T. H. Griffith]

As in Plato's *Republic,* the dividing of men into four classes was originally intended to suggest that human nature may quite naturally be divided into intellectuals and priests (*brahmins*); rulers, warriors, statesmen (*kshatriyas*); businessmen and managers (*vaishyas*); and workers and servants (*shūdras*) —and that a society as a whole functions best when each person in it knows his "place" and works within it for his own self-fulfillment and for the good of all.[5] Each "caste" has its appropriate responsibilities to society and its appropriate rights and privileges. Until such time as one abandons society and becomes a *sannyāsin,* one is obligated to work within the social structure. A man's position in society is determined by his nature, capacities, talents, and interests.

In sum, then, *dharma* refers to the norms which make a social order; to the duties of an individual in society with respect to his particular stage in life, his aims in life, and his class position—as this is determined ideally by his own natural capacities and mental-moral-spiritual development.

Brahman

The word *Brahman* first appears in the Rig Veda (*c.* 1200 B.C.) in the context of various utterances that were believed to have a special magical power. Originally, then, *Brahman* may have signified only "spell" or "prayer"—an invocation for the attainment of worldly wishes (rain, prosperity, fertility) and other worldly bliss. In some places *Brahman* was objectified and was regarded as arising from *rita* ("order," "truth") and as thus having a universal significance (Rig Veda VIII, 36, 1). Later, and as a development of this (e.g., Atharva Veda XI, 8, 32), *Brahman* came to signify that principle which stands behind the gods as their ground, and in the *Upanishads* generally it becomes the unitary, undifferentiated principle of all being, the knowledge of which liberates one from finitude.

In the *Gītā*, *Brahman* is used in several senses. In some passages it is used as a substitute for the term *prakriti* ("unconscious nature") and in others as a synonym for the term *Veda*. The general Upanishadic metaphysical meaning of *Brahman*, though, is retained and unless otherwise noted, it has this signification.

karma

The term *karma* means "deed," "work," "action" and is used in the Hindu tradition to mean both any action which produces tendencies or impressions (*san-skāras*) in the actor, which then function as determinants to his future action, and specific ritual actions which are performed in the context of Vedic ceremonial religion. Further, according to most of the Indian philosophical systems, *karma* suggests a "law" of moral nature which holds that actions necessarily produce effects and that this is enacted over a period of innumerable births, deaths, and rebirths. Every action must produce its results—if not immediately, then at some future time—and every disposition to act is the result of one's past action. One is completely responsible for oneself. A man's present condition is the result of his past action over many lives, and his future condition will result from his past and present action.[6]

guna

The concept of *guna*—"strand," "quality," "constituent"—was developed most fully in ancient Indian philosophy by the Sānkhya system, and it is the Sānkhyan meaning of the term (rather than that of other philosophical systems such as the Vaisheshika) which the *Gītā* generally follows. Nature (*prakriti*), according to Sānkhya, is composed of several basic strands or "energy fields" which are called *sattva* or "dynamic equilibrium," *rajas* or "turbulence," and *tamas* or "dullness." Everything in Nature represents some special combination of these three factors. The *gunas,* however, are taken, and especially in the *Gītā,* not only as fields or dimensions of physical Nature, but also as qualities of psychic being and moral consciousness. *Sattva* stands here for a preponderance of intelligence and objectivity and is considered to be "good"; *rajas* stands for a preponderance of emotion and subjectivity and is considered to be that which is capable of becoming either "good" or "bad," depending upon how and where it is directed (but in any case remains less good than *sattva*); and *tamas* stands for a preponderance of ignorance, insensibility, and lethargy and is judged to be "bad." The criterion of "good" and "bad" implicit in this context is: that which is most conducive to spiritual realization is "good"; that which most stands in its way is "bad."

According to the *Gītā*, men tend naturally toward various "types" which are founded on the relative distribution of the *gunas* within them. Men of a predominantly *sattvic* disposition are by their nature contemplative, philosophical, moral; men of a predominantly *rajasic* disposition tend to be active, ambitious, strong-willed; and those of a *tamasic* disposition tend to be slothful, dimwitted, and prone to simple sensuality. When the term *guna* is used in the *Gītā* it is necessary to look closely at the context in which it is employed in order to see whether the physical, psychological, or moral aspect is emphasized. When it refers primarily to physical Nature it suggests various energy states which constitute Nature and which are the locus of its order and "determinism"; [7] when it refers primarily to psychological dispositions and morality it suggests "character types" and basic volitional attitudes.[8]

jñāna

Jñāna means "knowledge," "intuition," "spiritual understanding," and is often used in conjunction with *yoga* to denote the spiritual path by means of which men of strong intellectual or philosophical (*sattvic*) disposition seek self-realization. *Jñāna yoga* is the discipline associated most closely with Advaita Vedānta, the non-dualistic system expounded primarily by Shankara. It demands a rigorous intellectual discrimination between the phenomenal world and the real world of Brahman, and culminates in an intuitive identification which shatters the independent existence of everything but the non-dual One. The *Gītā* speaks highly of this path but suggests that in its pure form it is meaningful for only a very few persons, and that by itself it cannot lead to the special sort of world-affirmation with which the *Gītā* is concerned.

bhakti

Bhakti means "love" or "devotion" and refers to that special intensity by which man reaches out to the Divine. *Bhakti* is the loving adoration for a personal divinity. Psychologically it may be said to represent a sublimation of passions, desires, emotions—their redirection from natural ends to a divine being—and an intensification of that natural religious emotion which seeks fulfillment through spiritual unity. *Bhakti* does not mean interpersonal human love or a love for man which follows from a love of God; it means, rather, an intense devotion which seeks to obtain unity with the Divine Being to whom the devotion is directed. *Bhakti*, when conjoined with *yoga*, thus means "the path of devotion." According to the *Gītā*, *bhakti yoga* is the means by which most persons are able to plumb the depths of religious experience.

māyā

The term *māyā* has a long history in Indian thought (it was used in the ancient Veda to signify a mysterious, deceptive power of the gods; e.g., Rig Veda, III, 53, 8; VI, 47, 18), and it has come to be associated primarily with the Advaita Vedānta of Shankara and to denote that which produces, and that which is, the world of our ordinary experience. According to the non-dualistic (*a-dvaita*) interpretation, the existence of, and our perception of, an independent substantial world of real objects, persons, and processes is grounded in a pervasive error. We take the unreal for the real and the real for the unreal. This fundamental error is then characterized as beginningless (*anādi*), for time arises only within it; as unthinkable (*acintya*), for all thought is subject to it; as indescribable (*anirvacanīya*), for all conceptual language results from it. It is said to embrace a twofold power—that of concealing reality (*āvarana-shakti*), and of misrepresenting or distorting it (*vikshepa-shakti*) ; in short, man not only fails to perceive reality, he also substitutes something else in its place, the phenomenal world.

This advaitic usage of *māyā,* however, is not fully accepted by the *Gītā.* The connotation of "illusion" which is attached to the term in Advaita Vedānta is present only to the extent of suggesting the status of Nature (*prakriti*) when it is taken by itself as an independent reality. For the most part in the *Gītā, māyā* denotes the power of the Divine to order Nature. Nature is the result of God's "creative power," of his *māyā,* and Nature has the power of deluding a man when, and insofar as, he takes it to be an independent ultimate reality.

III

Who Is Arjuna?

What ought I to do? What is my duty? For Arjuna, the "hero" of the *Bhagavad Gītā,* the questions have immediate existential import. Ought I to fight in a war in which my own kinsmen are in the opposing army, although it is a just war? In terms of the *Weltanschauung* which informs the dramatic events portrayed in the poem, however, a brotherhood of man exists by virtue of the indwelling presence of the Divine in man: one's own kinsmen are always in the opposing army. In generalized form, Arjuna's question may then be stated as: Ought I to perform an act which is injurious or even fatal to another person? or, Ought I to fulfill my social duty, which is itself determined by my past experience, in those actions which are morally repugnant to me? or, If I must perform an act which is distasteful to me but which is dictated by my duty and nature, in what spirit or attitude ought I to perform the act?

Arjuna is anyone who asks these questions, not so much in the abstract as at the moment when a concrete decision about a specific course of action is demanded.

IV

Krishna as an Avatāra

Krishna, in the *Bhagavad Gītā*, is the *guru* or spiritual teacher of Arjuna. Acting the role of Arjuna's charioteer, he presents him with a vision of the universe and sets forth various *yogas*; by following them, a man may realize this vision in his own experience. Krishna, though, is not just a human *guru*, rather he is a manifestation of Vishnu, the personal God, who is also identified with the *purushottama* or highest spiritual principle. Further, Krishna proclaims himself as a god who assumes a bodily form whenever there is a predominance of *adharma* or unrighteousness in the world, in order that *dharma* or righteousness may be re-established. This periodic incarnation of the Divine is called *avatārana* or the descent of the Divine in the world.

> Whenever there is a decay of righteousness and a rising up of unrighteousness, O Bhārata, I send forth Myself.
>
> [IV, 7]

> For the preservation of good, for the destruction of evil, for the establishment of righteousness, I come into being in age after age.
>
> [IV, 8]

But if one takes this doctrine of Krishna as an *avatāra* literally, one must acknowledge that it is simply inconsistent with the rest of the teaching about the nature of the Divine and the world which is put forward by the *Gītā*.[9] Nature, or *prakriti*, the *Gītā* suggests, is indifferent to the moral concerns of man. It acts out of the necessity of its own being. This *prakriti* is also called the "lower nature" of the Divine (VII, 4–5): it is a manifestation or expression of the Spirit in the world. Further, according to the general Hindu cosmological scheme which the poem accepts (VIII, 16–19; IX, 7–10), the world always runs a course from *dharma* to *adharma* and finally to a state of dissolution (*pralaya*), after which the cycle recommences. And this endless cyclical pattern is grounded in the Divine.

> . . . I am the origin of the whole world and also its dissolution.
>
> [VII, 6]

To complicate the picture even further, this "lower nature" of the Divine, which is subject to growth and decay, is referred to as *māyā*—that which results from the creative power of the Divine, and that which is "illusory" when seen as independent of the Divine.

Now it would certainly be odd if the Lord were to enter into his own lower nature whenever it goes astray —this lower nature, which is controlled by Him, is an illusion when seen as separate from Him, and is destined to dissolve—in order to adjust it for the benefit of those living beings whose primary duty is precisely to overcome all attachment to it!

If the *Gītā* is to have a consistent teaching, then, we must look for a deeper psychological or allegorical meaning in this doctrine of divine descent, and it is not too difficult to find one.

When a man comes to realize the extent of his bondage to the world and to his empirical self, and how he is a victim of external forces and internal desires and needs, at the same time it seems he realizes, however dimly, that he can be something other than he is. The realization of unrighteousness, *adharma,* implies some recognition of that which is opposed to it—righteousness or *dharma.* There is the recognition that one is essentially more than one actually is. This awareness also seems to carry with it a call or inner demand to reinstate one's higher self as the vital center of one's being. The "descent of the Divine into a bodily form" is an awakening to one's own higher potential; it is the inner demand to be redirected to spiritual being whenever one deviates from it. *Avatārana* is present whenever a man is empirically awakened to the fact of his spiritual status as a human being.

"All gods verily are the Self." [10] Philosophically, Krishna is thus Arjuna's own higher self calling for self-realization.

V

The Progressive Teaching Technique of the Gītā

In Chapter II of the *Gītā,* after unsuccessfully urging Arjuna out of his passivity and lethargy, Krishna proffers a series of arguments, some of which appeal to just those aspects of Arjuna's nature which bind him to "ignorance."

If you act contrary to your duty as a warrior you will only incur sin. And you will be dishonored. Your peers will think that you are a coward, and you will be talked about accordingly. You have nothing to lose by fighting. If you win the battle, you gain the fruits of the earth; if you lose and are killed you will go to heaven for having fulfilled your duty. [Paraphrased from II, 33–37]

Many readers of the poem have been somewhat taken aback by these arguments, which strike them either as inhumane or as merely appealing to the base desires of a warrior. Kill, because it is one's duty to do so! Kill, for otherwise one will incur sin! Kill, because if you don't you will be called a coward! Kill, because one has only to gain by doing so! And the *Bhagavad Gītā* is revered as a great religious text!

But with all these exclamations of horror, one simply misses or is insensitive to one of the standard techniques of teaching employed throughout the Indian philosophical-religious tradition. It is the technique, used at the beginning stages of the student's spiritual development, which seeks to bring about a desired spiritual end through means which we might judge as being not altogether "morally" appropriate to, or consistent with, that end (e.g., the use of intellectual "dishonesty"). In Indian philosophy the end does justify the means— *provided that the end is spiritual enlightenment.*[11]

The "progressive teaching" technique is a step-by-step leading of the self to higher levels of insight and understanding. It is founded, psychologically, on the belief that at any given time one is capable of grasping and assimilating only those ideas or arguments that are commensurate with one's achieved level of understanding. Just as mathematics is learned first in terms of symbols and principles that might later be negated or transformed in advanced studies, so in matters of the spirit a man begins with what he is capable of understanding, even though it will later be rejected.

One of the fine subtleties of the *Bhagavad Gītā* is

the extensive use made of this technique. Arjuna will be taught something by Krishna that is either aimed at his exact level of understanding (and prompts him to action wherein the teaching is fulfilled), or at a level of understanding somewhat beyond him but which he is able subsequently to assimilate into his experience. At still other times Arjuna will grasp intellectually some truths given to him but which, when they have become actual contents of his experience, turn out to be infinitely richer than he imagined. (Chapter X, for example, spells out discursively the complexity and ultimate simplicity of the Divine Nature. Arjuna grasps this but is nevertheless overwhelmed by the direct vision which is vouchsafed to him in the next chapter.) Spiritual experience, in short, not only fulfills but also transforms intellectual understanding.

In order to understand the *Gītā*, let alone to appreciate its artistic and spiritual efficacy, one must not take an argument, an appeal, a doctrine, out of its teaching context. The low-level arguments put forward in Chapter II serve merely to shake Arjuna out of his lethargy. They are justified, for Indian thought, by the spiritual results which they produce.[12]

Notes

1. A Kashmiri text of the *Bhagavad Gītā*, which is believed to be somewhat earlier than the text used by the classical philosophers in their commentaries, has been found by Professor F. Otto Schrader. The variations between these texts,

however, are minor and do not significantly alter the philo-sophical-religious teachings of the *Gītā*. Cf. Franklin Edger-ton's references to this in Vol. I of his *Bhagavad Gītā* (Cambridge: Harvard University Press, 1952), p. xiii.

2. It is often suggested that the *Gītā* represents a synthesis between the āryan Brahmanic tradition (of the Vedic *Sanhitās, Brāhmanas, Āranyakas, Upanishads,* and somewhat later *Dharma-shāstras*) and the popular, indigenous culture of pre-āryan India. The cult of Krishna, in this account, is basically non-Brahmanic in origin and spirit, as are many of the pronounced "theistic" dimensions of the *Gītā* as a whole. Together with the hieratic, ritualistic Brahmanic tradition, and no doubt preceding it in time, there were in India a large number of "tribal" religions. These, it is generally believed, emphasized a spirit/body dualism and a consequent asceticism, and this may be sharply contrasted with the worldly optimism of the early āryan invaders. Hinduism is then looked upon as a synthesis of Brahmanic and popular culture. It incorporates the ritualistic, sacrificial elements of the early Veda, the more abstract, introspective philosophical concerns of the *Upanishads,* and the dualistic body/spirit, man/God relationships of popular culture.

This notion of Hinduism in general, and the *Bhagavad Gītā* in particular, as being a synthesis of Brahmanic and indigenous thought is no doubt correct in a number of essential points. Until a much greater knowledge and understanding is obtained, however, about the non-āryan cultures of ancient India, it is perhaps best to see the main lines of the *Gītā*'s philosophy, and the technical terms in which these are expressed, as a continuation and expansion of Brahmanic culture *per se.*

3. The oldest text which is available on Sānkhya is the *Sānkhya-Kārikā* by Īshvarakrishna, written in the third century A.D. It has been handed down with a commentary by Gaudapāda (about whom there is a great deal of uncertainty), and several English translations of this work have been made. Vācaspati's commentary, the *Sānkhyatattvakaumudī,* written in the ninth century, is also considered an authoritative work in this tradition. Several translations of this work have been made. For a good introduction to the

system in its historical relations with other Indian systems, A. B. Keith's *The Sānkhya System* (London: Oxford University Press, 1918) is recommended.

4. In actual practice, only a relatively few orthodox Hindus make the effort demanded by this stage Sannyāsins are many in India, but they are considerably outnumbered by those who see in the third stage the fulfillment of their *dharma*.

   The student is advised to consult any of the standard reference works on Hinduism, or better, the *Laws of Manu* itself, for a more complete description of the *āshramas* and the precise duties which each enjoin upon members of the different social classes.

5. The *shūdras* were in actuality more of an "outcaste" than a class within the fold, for they were, and are, denied participation in the Vedic rituals and sacraments. They are not, though, to be confused with the "untouchables," who are not mentioned anywhere in the text.

6. For a more detailed description of *karma* and its logical status in Vedānta, see the author's "Karma as a 'Convenient Fiction' in Advaita Vedānta," *Philosophy East and West*, XV (1965), 3–12.

7. E.g., III, 5, 28, 29; XIV, 5 ff.

8. E.g., VII, 12; XIV, 17 ff.; XVII, 4 ff.

9. We are not concerned here with the religious dimensions or mythological value, as such, of the doctrine of *avatāras* as embodied in Vaishnavism, but only with its philosophical status in the *Bhagavad Gītā*. It is not our intention, in other words, to question the adequacy of this doctrine in the sectarian context of Hinduism but to understand its place and significance in the *Gītā*.

   For a description of the historical origins and roles of Krishna in Hinduism, see John Dawson, *Hindu Mythology* (London: Routledge & Kegan Paul Ltd., 1961), pp. 160–168, and *Krishna: Myths, Rites, and Attitudes*, edited by Milton Singer (Honolulu: East-West Center Press, 1966).

10. *Manu*, XII, 119.

11. Cf. for example in Buddhism, the "Parable of the Burning House" in *Saddharma Pandarīka*.

12. Reading the *Gītā* as a series of "progressive teachings" might also help to explain the very presence of the last chapters in the text. Readers are often surprised to discover that the text does not end at Chapter XII or XIII, for the subsequent chapters seem anticlimactic and considerably less profound than preceding ones. An answer to this difficulty is perhaps that Arjuna, after having been given a vision of the Divine, needs to relearn something about the nature of the ordinary world of everyday experience. Arjuna is to work in the world, and if he fails to understand its "demoniac" as well as higher potentialities he may labor under the delusion that the world is easily redeemed. It is also likely that Arjuna may forget the world completely after his great vision, or be filled with pride for having received it. He is thus brought back to the world; it and his position in it are explained to him, and he is then ready to act.

English Translation

CHAPTER

I

Arjuna's Depression

Dhritarāshtra [1] said:

What did the sons of Pāndu [2] and my men do, O   1
Sanjaya,[3] when, eager to fight, they gathered together on the field of righteousness, the Kuru
field? [4]

Sanjaya said:

When seeing the army of the Pāndavas drawn   2
up in battle array, Duryodhana the prince ap-
proached his teacher (Drona [5]) and spoke these
words:

Behold, O teacher, this mighty army of the sons   3
of Pāndu arrayed by thy skillful pupil, the son of
Drupada.[6]

Here are heroes, great archers, in battle they are   4
equal to Arjuna and Bhīma—Yuyudhāna [7] and
Virāta [8] and Drupada of the great chariot;

Dhrishtaketu,[9] Cekitāna [10] and the valiant King 5
of Kāshi (Benares), also Purijit,[11] Kuntibhoja [12]
and Shaibya,[13] the best of men;

Yudhāmanyu [14] the valiant and Uttamaujas [15] 6
the brave, the son of Subhadrā [16] and the sons of
Draupadī,[17] all great warriors indeed.

Know also, O best of the twice-born, the lead- 7
ers of my army. I name those that are most distinguished for thy recognition.

Thyself (Drona) and Bhīshma [18] and Karna [19] 8
and Kripa,[20] the victorious in battle; Asvatthāman [21] and Vikarna [22] and also the son of Somadatta.[23]

And many other heroes who are willing to risk 9
their lives for my sake. Armed with various weapons, they are all skilled in war.

Although this army of ours seems insufficient,[24] 10
it is protected by Bhīshma; while their army, which
seems sufficient, is protected by Bhīma.

Therefore in all fronts, stationed in your respec- 11
tive ranks, guard ye Bhīshma above all.

The aged (oldest) grandson of the Kurus 12
(Bhīshma), bringing joy to him (Duryodhana),
blew his conch shell and roared a lion's roar on
high.

Then conches and kettledrums, cymbals and 13
drums and horns suddenly were struck and the
sound was tumultuous.

Then stationed in their great chariot, which was 14
yoked to white horses, Mādhava (Krishna) and
the son of Pāndu (Arjuna) blew their wondrous
conch shells.

Krishna blew Pāñcajanya and Arjuna (blew) 15
Devadatta, and Bhīma, of terrible deeds, blew his
mighty conch Paundra.

The King Yudhishthira, the son of Kuntī, 16
(blew) Anantavijaya, and Nakula and Sahadeva
(blew) Sughosha and Manipushpaka.

And the King of Kāshi, the excellent archer; 17
Shikandim, the great warrior; Dhrishtadyumna
and Virāta and the unconquered Sātyaki;

Drupada and the sons of Drupadī, O Lord of the 18
earth, and the strong-armed son of Subhadrā, on
all sides blew their respective conches.

The tumultuous noise, resounding through earth 19
and sky, rent the hearts of the sons of Dhritarāshtra.

Then Arjuna, who bore the crest of the god 20
Hanumān, seeing the sons of Dhritarāshtra standing arrayed, as the discharge of weapons began,
took up his bow,

And to Hrishīkesha (Krishna), then, O Lord of   21
earth, he spoke these words: Stop my chariot, O
immovable one, between the two armies,

That I may behold these men standing eager   22
for battle, with whom I must fight in this strife of
war;

And see those who are assembled here, ready to   23
fight, and who are desirous of pleasing in battle
the evil-minded son of Dhritarāshtra.

Thus addressed by Gudākesha (Arjuna), Hrishī-   24
kesha (Krishna), O Bhārata, placed that excellent
chariot between the two armies.

And in front of Bhīshma and Drona and all the   25
kings, he said: Behold O Pārtha (Arjuna) these assembled Kurus.

Arjuna saw standing there fathers and grand-   26
fathers, teachers, uncles, brothers, sons and grandsons, and also companions;

And fathers-in-law and friends in both the ar-   27
mies. Seeing all these kinsmen thus arrayed, the son
of Kuntī (Arjuna),

Filled with the utmost compassion, sorrowfully   28
spoke: Seeing my own kinsmen, O Krishna, arrayed
and wishing to fight,

My limbs collapse, my mouth dries up, there is   29
trembling in my body and my hair stands on end;

(The bow) Gāndīva slips from my hand and my   30
skin also is burning; I am not able to stand still, my
mind is whirling.

And I see evil portents, O Keshava (Krishna),   31
and I foresee no good in slaying my own kinsmen
in the fight.

I do not desire victory, O Krishna, nor kingdom,   32
nor pleasure. Of what use is kingdom to us, O
Govinda (Krishna), of what use pleasure or life?

Those for whose sake we desire kingdom, pleas-   33
ures and happiness, they are arrayed here in battle,
having renounced their lives and riches.

Teachers, fathers, sons, and also grandfathers;   34
uncles, fathers-in-law, grandsons, brothers-in-law
and (other) kinsmen:

These I do not wish to kill, though they kill me,   35
O Madhusūdana (Krishna); even for the kingdom
of the three worlds; how (much less) then for the
sake of the earth!

What pleasure can be ours, O Janārdana   36
(Krishna) in slaying the sons of Dhritarāshtra?
Only evil would attach to us if we kill these felons.

Therefore we should not slay the sons of   37
Dhritarāshtra, our kinsmen. How could we be
happy killing our own people, O Mādhava?

Even if they, whose minds are destroyed by 3ᴜ greed, do not see the sin caused by the destruction of a family and the crime incurred in the injury to a friend;

Why should we not have the wisdom to turn 39 back from this sin, we who see the evil in the destruction of the family, O Janārdana (Krishna)?

In the ruin of a family, its immemorial laws per- 40 ish; and when the laws perish, the whole family is overcome by lawlessness.

And when lawlessness prevails, O Krishna, the 41 women of the family are corrupted, and when women are corrupted, O Vārshneya, a mixture of caste arises.

And this confusion brings the family itself to 42 hell and those who have destroyed it; for their ancestors fall, deprived of their offerings of rice and water.

By the sins of those who destroy a family and 43 create a mixture of caste, the eternal laws of the caste and the family are destroyed.

The men of the families whose laws are de- 44 stroyed, O Janārdana, assuredly will dwell in hell; so we have heard.

Alas, what a great sin we resolved to commit in 45 undertaking to kill our own people through our greed for the pleasures of kingdom.

It would be better for me if the sons of Dhritar- 46
āshtra, with weapons in hand, should slay me, un-
resisting and unarmed, in the battle.

Having spoken thus on the battlefield, Arjuna 47
cast away his bow and arrow and sank down on the
seat of his chariot, his spirit overcome by grief.

*

In the famous Upanishad *of the* Bhagavadgītā, *the
knowledge of Brahman, the scripture of yoga, and the
dialogue between Shrī Krishna and Arjuna, this is the
first chapter, entitled "The Yoga of Arjuna's Depression"* (arjunavishādayoga) .

CHAPTER

II

The Yoga of Knowledge

Sanjaya said:

To him who was thus overcome by pity, whose   1
troubled eyes were filled with tears, and who was
despondent, Madhusūdana (Krishna) spoke these
words:

The Blessed Lord said:

Whence hath this despair come to thee in this   2
(time of) crisis? It is unbecoming to an *āryan*,[1] it
does not lead to heaven, it is disgraceful, O Arjuna.

Yield not to this impotence, O Pārtha (Arjuna),   3
for it is not proper of thee. Abandon this petty
weakness of heart and arise, O oppressor of the foe.

Arjuna said:

How, O Madhusūdana (Krishna), shall I attack,   4
with arrows in battle, Bhīshma and Drona who are
worthy of worship, O slayer of enemies?

It would be better (to live) in this world by 5
begging than to slay these noble teachers. For by
slaying these teachers who desire wealth, I would
enjoy only blood-smeared delights.

We do not know which is better for us, whether 6
we should conquer them or they should conquer us.
There standing before us are the sons of Dhritarāshtra; if we were to slay them, we should not
wish to live.

My being is afflicted with the defect of pity; my 7
mind is confused about my *dharma*. I ask Thee:
tell me decisively which is better. I am Thy pupil;
teach me, who seeks refuge in Thee.

I do not see what can drive away this sorrow 8
which parches my senses even if I obtained a rich
and unrivaled kingdom on earth, or even the sover-
eignty of the gods.

Sanjaya said:
The mighty Gudākesha (Arjuna), having thus 9
addressed Hrishīkesha (Krishna), said to Govinda (Krishna), "I will not fight," and fell
silent.

Then, O Bhārata (Dhritarāshtra), Hrishīkesha 10
(Krishna), smiling as it were, spoke these words
to him who was despondent in the midst of the
two armies.

The Blessed Lord said:
Thou grievest for those thou shouldst not grieve 11

for, and yet thou speakest words that sound like wisdom.[2] Wise men do not mourn for the dead or for the living.

Never was there a time when I did not exist, nor thou, nor these rulers of men; nor will there ever be a time hereafter when we shall all cease to be. 12

As the soul [3] in this body passes through childhood, youth and old age, so (after departure from this body) it passes on to another body. The sage is not bewildered by this. 13

Contacts with the objects of the senses,[4] O son of Kuntī (Arjuna), give rise to cold and heat, pleasure and pain. They come and go, they are impermanent; endure them, O Bhārata (Arjuna). 14

The man who is not troubled by these (contacts), O bull among men (Arjuna), who treats alike pleasure and pain, who is wise; he is fit for immortality.[5] 1

Of non-being there is no coming to be; of being [6] there is no ceasing to be. The truth about both is seen by the seers of truth. 1

Know that by which all this is pervaded is indestructible,[7] and that no one can cause the destruction of this immutable [8] being. 17

It is said that (only) these bodies of the eternal [9] embodied (soul), which is indestructible [10] and in- 18 comprehensible,[11] are perishable.[12] Therefore fight, O Bhārata (Arjuna) !

He who thinks that this (soul) is a slayer, and he   19
who thinks that this (soul) is slain; both of them
are ignorant. This (soul) neither slays nor is slain.[13]

It is never born, nor does it die, nor having once   20
been, will it again cease to be. It is unborn,[14] eternal and everlasting.[15] This primeval one is not slain
when the body is slain.

He who knows that it (the soul) is indestructible   21
and eternal, unborn and unchanging, how can that
man slay, O Pārtha (Arjuna), or cause another to
slay?

Just as a man casts off worn-out clothes and takes   22
on others that are new, so the embodied soul casts
off worn-out bodies [16] and takes on others that are
new.

Weapons do not cut it, nor does fire burn it;   23
waters do not make it wet, nor does wind make it
dry.

It is uncleavable, it cannot be burnt, it can be   24
neither wetted nor dried. It is eternal, omnipresent,[17] unchanging [18] and immovable.[19] It is everlasting.

It is called unmanifest,[20] unthinkable [21] and im-   25
mutable; [22] therefore, knowing it as such, thou
shouldst not grieve.

Even if thou thinkest that it is constantly born 26
and constantly dies, even then, O mighty-armed
(Arjuna), thou shouldst not grieve.

For death is certain for one that has been born, 27
and birth is certain for one that has died. Therefore
for what is unavoidable, thou shouldst not grieve.

All beings are unmanifest in their beginnings, 28
they are manifest in their middles and are unmanifest again in their ends, O Bhārata (Arjuna). What
(reason) is there, then, for lamentation?

One sees it as marvelous, another also speaks of it 29
as marvelous, another hears of it as marvelous, but
even after having heard (of it), no one whatsoever
knows it.

The soul in the body of everyone, O Bhārata 30
(Arjuna), is eternal and indestructible.[23] Therefore
thou shouldst not mourn for any creature.

Further, having regard for thine own *dharma*, 31
thou shouldst not tremble. There exists no greater
good for a Kshatriya than a battle required by duty.

Happy are the Kshatriyas, O Pārtha (Arjuna), 32
for whom such a battle comes by mere chance,
opening the door to heaven.

But if thou wilt not wage this righteous battle, 33
then having thrown away thy duty and glory, thou
wilt incur sin.[24]

Besides, men will forever speak of thy dishonor, 34
and for one who has been honored, dishonor is
worse than death.

The great warriors will think that thou hast ab- 35
stained from battle because of fear and they who
highly esteemed thee will think lightly of thee.

Many words which ought not to be spoken will 36
be spoken by thy enemies, scorning thy strength.
What is more painful than that?

If thou art slain, thou wilt obtain heaven, or if 37
thou conquer, thou wilt enjoy the earth. Therefore
arise, O son of Kuntī, resolved to fight.

Regarding alike pleasure and pain, gain and loss, 38
victory and defeat, prepare thyself for battle. Thus
thou wilt not incur sin.

This is the wisdom of the *sānkhya* which has 39
been declared to thee, O Pārtha. Listen now to the
wisdom of the yoga; when disciplined with it, thou
shalt cast away the bondage of *karma*.

In this path there is no loss of effort and no harm 40
occurs. Even a little of this *dharma* protects one
from great fear.

The resolute understanding is clearly directed in 41
this, O joy of the Kurus, but the thoughts of the
irresolute are many-branched and endless.

The ignorant, O Pārtha, whose selves consist of 42
desire, who are intent (only) on reaching heaven, 43
and who say there is nothing else, rejoice in the
letter of the Veda and utter those flowery words
which give rise to many ritual performances for the
attainment of enjoyment and power, but which result in rebirth as the fruit of these actions.

The intelligence [25] of those (who are intended to 44
have) resolute understanding (but) who are attached to enjoyment and power, and whose minds
are carried away by these (words), is not established in concentration.[26]

The Vedas deal with the activity of the three 45
gunas; but be thou, O Arjuna, free from the three
gunas and from the pairs [27] of opposites. Be thou
constantly fixed in *sattva*: not caring for the possession of property,[28] be self-possessed.

As much use as there is for a pond when there is 46
everywhere a flood, so much is there in all the Vedas
for a Brahmin who understands.

In action only hast thou a right and never in its 47
fruits.[29] Let not thy motive be the fruits of action;
nor let thy attachment be to inaction.

Fixed in yoga, O winner of wealth, perform ac- 48
tions, abandoning attachment and remaining even-
minded in success and failure; for serenity [30] of
mind is called yoga.

(Mere) action is far inferior to the discipline of 49
intelligence,[31] O winner of wealth. Seek refuge in
intelligence; pitiful are those whose motive is the
fruit (of action).

One who has disciplined his intelligence leaves 50
behind in this world both good and evil deeds.
Therefore strive for yoga, for yoga is skill in action.[32]

Having disciplined their intelligence and hav- 51
ing abandoned the fruit born of their action, the
wise are freed from the bondage of birth and attain
the state that is free from sorrow.

When thy intelligence shall cross the tangle of 52
delusion, then thou shalt become indifferent to
what shall be heard and to what has been heard (in
the Veda).

When thy intelligence, which is now perplexed 53
by the Vedic texts, shall stand immovable and be
fixed in concentration, then shalt thou attain yoga.

Arjuna said:
What is the description of the man of steady 54
mind [33] who is fixed in concentration, O Keshava
(Krishna)? How might the man of steady mind
speak, how might he sit, how might he walk?

The Blessed Lord said:
When a man abandons all the desires [34] of his 55

mind, O Pārtha (Arjuna), and is satisfied in his self [35] by the self alone, then he is called a man of steady mind.

He whose mind is not troubled in sorrow, and 56 has no desire in pleasure, his passion, fear and anger departed, he is called a steady-minded sage.

He who is not attached [36] to anything, who nei- 57 ther delights [37] nor is upset [38] when he obtains good or evil, his mind is firmly established (in wisdom).

And when he completely withdraws his senses [39] 58 from the objects of sense, as a tortoise draws in his limbs, his mind is firmly established.

The objects of sense,[40] but not the taste for them, 59 fall away from the embodied soul who abstains from food. Even the taste falls away from him when the Supreme [41] is seen.

The excited senses of even a wise man who strives 60 (for perfection), O son of Kuntī, violently carry away his mind.

Having restrained them all, he should sit disci- 61 plined, intent on Me; for his mind is firmly set whose senses are under control.

When a man dwells on the objects of sense, at- 62 tachment [42] to them is produced. From attachment desire arises, and from desire anger comes.

From anger arises delusion, from delusion loss of   63
memory, from loss of memory the destruction of
intelligence, and from the destruction of intelligence, he perishes.

But he who moves among the objects of sense,   64
with the senses under control and is free from desire and aversion, he who is thus self-controlled
attains serenity [43] of mind.

And in that serenity, the destruction of all pain   65
is produced for him. The intelligence of the man
of tranquil mind is quickly established.

For the uncontrolled, there is no intelligence,   66
nor for the uncontrolled is there concentration; [44]
and without concentration there is no peace, and
for the unpeaceful, how can there be happiness?

When the mind hastens after the roving senses,   67
it carries along the understanding, as wind carries
away a ship on the waters.

Therefore, O mighty-armed (Arjuna), his intel-   68
ligence is firmly established whose senses are completely withdrawn from the objects of sense.

What is night for all beings is the time of waking   69
for the man of self-control, and when all beings are
awake, that is night for the sage who sees.

He attains peace into whom all desires flow as   70
waters into the sea which, though ever being filled,

is ever motionless; and not he who lusts after desires.

He who abandons all desires and acts without longing, without self-interest or egotism, he attains peace.   71

This is the eternal state, O Pārtha (Arjuna); having attained it, one is no longer confused. Fixed in it even at the time of death, one attains to the bliss [45] of Brahman.   72

*

This is the second chapter, entitled "The Yoga of Knowledge" (sānkhyayoga).

CHAPTER

III

The Yoga of Action

Arjuna said:

If it be thought by Thee, O Janārdana (Krishna), 1
that (the path of) knowledge is superior to (the
path of) action, then why dost Thou urge me, O
Keshava (Krishna), in this terrible deed?

With these apparently equivocal words, Thou 2
confusest my understanding. Therefore tell me decisively the one path by which I may attain to the
good.

The Blessed Lord said:

In this world, O blameless one, a twofold path 3
has been taught before by Me; the path of knowledge (*jñāna yoga*) for men of discrimination
(*sānkhyas*) and the path of works (*karma yoga*)
for men of action (*yogins*).

Not by abstention from actions does a man gain 4
freedom, and not by mere renunciation does he attain perfection.

No one can remain, even for a moment, without   5
performing some action. Everyone is made to act
helplessly by the *gunas* born of *prakriti*.

He who controls his organs of action,[1] but   6
dwells [2] in his mind on the objects of the senses;
that man is deluded and is called a hypocrite.

But he who controls the senses by the mind, O   7
Arjuna, and, without attachment, engages the organs of action in *karma yoga*, he excels.

Perform thy allotted [3] work, for action is supe-   8
rior to inaction; even the maintenance of thy body
cannot be accomplished without action.

This world is in bondage to *karma*, unless *karma*   9
is performed for the sake of sacrifice.[4] For the sake
of that, O son of Kuntī, perform thy action free
from attachment.

In ancient times Prajāpati [5] created men to-   10
gether with sacrifice and said: By this shall ye pro-
create, let this be the granter of your desires.[6]

By this nourish ye the gods and may the gods   11
nourish thee; thus nourishing each other, ye shall
attain to the highest good.

Nourished by sacrifice, the gods will give thee   12
the enjoyments ye desire. He who enjoys what is
given by them without giving to them in return is
verily a thief.

The good men who eat the remains of the sacri- 13
fice (who share their food with others) are freed
from all sins; but wicked men who cook for their
own sake, verily they eat sin.

From food creatures come into being; from rain 14
food is produced, from sacrifice comes rain, and
sacrifice is born of action.

Know that (ritual) action arises from Brahman 15
(the Veda), and that Brahman arises from the Imperishable.[7] Therefore, Brahman, the all-pervading,
is ever established in sacrifice.

He who does not follow here on earth the wheel 16
thus set in motion is evil, O Pārtha; delighting in
the senses, he lives in vain.

But the man whose pleasure is in the Self alone, 17
who is pleased with the Self, who is content only in
the Self, for him there is no work that needs to be
done.

He has no interest [8] in action done in this world, 18
nor any with action not done. He is not dependent
on all these creatures for any object (of his).

Therefore, always perform the work that has to 19
be done without attachment, for man attains the
Supreme by performing work without attachment.

Janaka and others attained to perfection [9] only 20
by action; thou shouldst perform action also with
regard for the maintenance of the world.[10]

Whatsoever the best man does, other men do too. 21
Whatever standard [11] he sets, that the world follows.

There is nothing in the three worlds, O Pārtha, 22
to be done by Me, nor anything unobtained that
needs to be obtained; yet I continue in action.

For if I, unwearied, were not always in action, O 23
Pārtha, men everywhere would follow my path
(example).

If I did not perform action, these worlds would 24
be destroyed, and I should be the author of confusion and would destroy these people.

As the ignorant act with attachment to their 25
work, O Bhārata, so the wise man should act (but)
without attachment, desiring to maintain the order
of the world.

Let no wise man unsettle the minds of the igno- 26
rant who are attached to action. Acting with discipline, he should make all action attractive.

All actions are performed by the *gunas* of *pra-* 27
kriti alone. But he who is deluded by egoism [12]
thinks, "I am the doer."

He who knows the true essence [13] of the separa- 28
tion (of the soul) from both the *gunas* and action,[14]
O mighty-armed one, and that it is the *gunas* which
act upon the *gunas*, he is not attached (to action).

Those who are deluded by the *gunas* of *prakriti* 29
are attached to the action of the *gunas*. But the man
who knows the whole should not unsettle the ignorant who know only a part.[15]

Surrendering all actions to Me, with thy con- 30
sciousness (fixed) on the supreme Self,[16] being free
from desire and selfishness, fight freed from thy sorrow.

They who constantly follow My doctrine,[17] who 31
are filled with faith [18] and are uncomplaining, they
too are freed from (the bondage of) actions.

But those who carp at my teaching and do not 32
follow it, know these mindless ones, deluded in all
knowledge, to be lost.

Even the wise man acts in conformity with his 33
own nature. Beings follow nature. What will restraint accomplish?

Attraction and repulsion for the objects of sense 34
are seated in the senses. Let no one come under the
control of these two; they are his enemies.

Better one's own *dharma*, though imperfect, 35
than another's well performed. Better death in (the
fulfillment of) one's own law, for another's law is
dangerous.

Arjuna said:
Then by what is a man impelled to (commit) 36

sin against his will, as if compelled [19] by force, O Vārshneya?

The Blessed Lord said:
It is desire, it is wrath, born of the *guna* of   37
passion (*rajas*), all-devouring and very sinful.
Know that this is the enemy here.

As fire is covered by smoke, as a mirror by dust,   38
and as an embryo is enveloped by the womb, so this
(knowledge) is covered by that (passion).

Knowledge is enveloped, O son of Kuntī, by this   39
constant enemy of the knower, by this insatiable
flame of desire.

The senses, the mind (*manas*), the understand-   40
ing (*buddhi*), are said to be its basis.[20] With these
it bewilders the embodied soul, covering its knowledge.

Therefore, O best of the Bharatas, having in the   41
beginning controlled thy senses, slay this evil destroyer of spiritual (*jñāna*) and practical (*vijñāna*)
knowledge.[21]

The senses, they say, are great; greater than the   42
senses is the mind (*manas*); greater than the mind
is the reason (*buddhi*); and greater than the reason
is He.

Thus having known that which is greater than   43
the reason, steadying the self by the self, slay the

enemy, O mighty-armed one, (that has) the form
of desire, and that is so hard to approach.

*

This is the third chapter, entitled "The Yoga of Action"
(karmayoga) .

CHAPTER

IV

The Yoga of Knowledge

The Blessed Lord said:

This imperishable yoga I proclaimed to Vivas-   1
vant; Vivasvant told it to Manu and Manu spoke
it to Ikshvāku.

Thus received in regular succession, the royal   2
sages knew it, till over a long passage of time this
yoga was lost to the world, O oppressor of the foe.

This same ancient yoga is declared today by Me   3
to thee, for thou art My devotee and friend, and
this is a supreme secret.

Arjuna said:

Later was Thy birth, earlier was the birth of   4
Vivasvant. How may I understand this, that Thou
didst declare it (to him) in the beginning?

The Blessed Lord said:

Many are My past lives and thine, O Arjuna; I   5

know all of them but thou knowest them not, O oppressor of the foe.

Although unborn, although My self is imperish- 6
able, although I am Lord of all beings, yet establishing Myself in My own (material) nature, I
come into being by My own mysterious power
(*māyā*).

Whenever there is a decay of righteousness and a 7
rising up of unrighteousness, O Bhārata, I send
forth Myself.

For the preservation of good, for the destruction 8
of evil, for the establishment of righteousness, I
come into being in age after age.[1]

He who thus truly knows My divine birth and 9
actions is not born again on leaving the body but
comes to Me, O Arjuna.

Freed from passion, fear and anger, filled with 10
Me, taking refuge in Me, many who are purified by
the austerity[2] of wisdom (*jñāna*) have come to My
state of being.

In whatever way men approach Me, I am gra- 11
cious to them; men everywhere, O Pārtha, follow
My path.

Those who desire the success which comes from 12
ritual actions sacrifice to the gods in this world; for
in the world of men success comes quickly from
such acts.

The four-caste system ³ was created by Me by the   13
division of *guna* and *karma*. Although I am the
maker of this, know Me as the imperishable non-
doer.

Actions do not stain Me; for I have no longing   14
for their fruits. He who knows Me thus is not
bound by actions.

The ancients who were desirous of liberation and   15
who knew this did their work. Therefore perform
action as the ancients did long ago.

What is action? What is inaction? About this   16
even the wise are confused. Therefore I will declare to thee what action is, knowing which thou
shalt be freed from evil.⁴

One must understand (the nature of) action,   17
and one must understand (the nature of) wrong
action, and one must understand (the nature of)
inaction: hard to understand is the way of action.

He who sees inaction in action and action in   18
inaction, he is wise among men; he does all actions
harmoniously.⁵

He whose undertakings are all free from desire   19
and will,⁶ whose actions are burned up in the fire
of knowledge, him the wise call learned.

Having abandoned attachment to the fruits of   20
action, always content and independent, he does
nothing even though he is engaged in action.

Having no desires, with his mind and self con- 21
trolled, abandoning all possessions, performing action with the body alone, he commits no sin.[7]

He who is content with what comes by chance, 22
who has passed beyond the pairs (of opposites),
who is free from jealousy and is indifferent to success and failure, even when he is acting he is not
bound.

The action of a man who is rid of attachment, 23
who is liberated, whose mind is firmly established
in knowledge, who performs action as a sacrifice, is
completely dissolved.

The offering is Brahman, Brahman is the obla- 24
tion; it is poured by Brahman in the (ritual) fire
of Brahman. Brahman is to be attained by him who
concentrates his actions upon Brahman.

Some yogins offer sacrifice to the deities; others 25
offer sacrifices by the sacrifice itself[8] in the fire of
Brahman.

Others offer hearing and the other senses into 26
the fires of restraint; others offer sound and the
other objects of sense into the fires of the senses.

Others offer up all the actions of the senses and 27
the actions of the vital breath into the fire of the
yoga of self-restraint that is kindled by knowledge.

Others offer as sacrifice their wealth or their aus- 28
terities or their yogic exercises, while still others of

restrained minds and difficult vows offer their study
(of the Veda) and their knowledge (of it).

Others who are intent upon breath control, hav- 29
ing restrained the paths of the outgoing and incoming breath, offer up the outgoing breath into the incoming breath and the incoming breath into the
outgoing breath.

Others, restricting their food, offer as sacrifice 30
their life breaths into life breaths. All these are
knowers of sacrifice, and their sins [9] are destroyed
by sacrifice.

Those who eat the life-giving remains of the sac- 31
rifice go to the eternal Brahman. Not even this
world is for the non-sacrificer, how then the next
world, O best of the Kurus?

Thus manifold sacrifices are spread out in the 32
face of Brahman. Know that they all are born of
action. Knowing this thou shalt be freed.

The sacrifice of knowledge is better than the sac- 33
rifice of material things, O scorcher of the foe. All
action, without exception, is completely terminated [10] in knowledge, O Pārtha.

Learn it by obeisance (to those who know), by 34
questioning and by serving them. The wise, the
seers of truth, will teach thee knowledge.

Knowing this thou shalt not fall again into de- 35
lusion, O Pāndava; for by this thou shalt see all
creatures without exception in the Self and in Me.

Even if thou art among sinners the worst sinner 36
of all, thou shalt cross over all evil by the boat of
knowledge alone.

As the fire which is kindled makes its fuel into 37
ashes, O Arjuna, so the fire of knowledge makes all
actions into ashes.

There is no purifier [11] in this world equal to wis- 38
dom. He who is perfected in yoga finds it in the self
in the course of time.

He who has faith, who is intent on it (knowledge) 39
and who has controlled his senses, obtains knowledge and having obtained it, goes quickly to the
highest peace.

But the ignorant man who is without faith and 40
of a doubting [12] nature perishes. For the doubting
self, there is not this world, nor the next, nor happiness.

Actions do not bind him who has renounced ac- 41
tions in yoga, who has cast away doubt by knowledge, who possesses himself, O winner of wealth.

Therefore having cut away, with the sword of 42
knowledge, this doubt in thy heart that is born of
ignorance, resort to yoga and arise, O Bhārata.

*

*This is the fourth chapter, entitled "The Yoga of Knowl-
edge"* (jñānayoga) .

CHAPTER

V

The Yoga of the Renunciation of Action

Arjuna said:

Thou praisest renunciation [1] of actions, O 1
Krishna, and again (*karma*) yoga. Tell me definitely which one of these is the better.

The Blessed Lord said:

Renunciation (of works) and the unselfish per- 2
formance of works (*karma yoga*) both lead to the
highest happiness. But of these two the unselfish
performance of works is better than the renunciation of works.

He who neither hates nor desires should be 3
known as the eternal renouncer; [2] free from the
pairs of opposites, O mighty-armed one, he is easily
released from bondage.

Children, not the wise, speak of renunciation 4
(*sānkhya*) and (*karma*) yoga as separate; for he

who is well established in one obtains the fruit of
both.

That place which is obtained by the *sānkhyas* is   5
also gained by the yogins. He who sees that *sānkhya*
and yoga are one, he truly sees.

Renunciation, O mighty-armed one, is difficult   6
to attain without yoga. The sage who is disciplined
in yoga soon goes to Brahman.

He who is disciplined in yoga and is pure in soul,   7
who is ruler of his self, who has conquered his
senses, whose self becomes the Self of all beings, he
is not affected by acting.

The disciplined one who knows the truth thinks   8
"I am doing nothing at all." In seeing, hearing,
touching, smelling, tasting, walking, sleeping,
breathing,

In speaking, giving, grasping, opening and clos-   9
ing the eyes, he maintains that only the senses are
active among the objects of the senses.

He who acts, having placed his actions in Brah-   10
man [3] and having abandoned attachment, is not
affected by sin, just as a lotus leaf is not affected by
water.

Yogins perform action only with the body, the   11
mind, the intellect or the senses, without attachment, for self-purification.

The disciplined man, having abandoned the 12
fruit of action, obtains enduring peace; the undisciplined man, impelled by desire, is attached to
the fruit and is bound.

Renouncing all actions of the mind, the sover- 13
eign embodied (soul) sits happily in the city of
nine gates,[4] neither acting nor causing action.

The sovereign Self [5] does not create agency (for 14
the people) of the world, nor actions, nor the conjunction of actions with their fruit. But nature itself operates there.

The all-pervading Spirit [6] does not take on the 15
sin or good work of anyone. Knowledge is enveloped by ignorance; by this creatures are bewildered.

But for those in whom ignorance is destroyed 16
by knowledge, for them knowledge illumines the
highest Self like the sun.

Thinking on that (highest Self), their self fixed 17
on that, established in that, devoted to that, they
go to wherefrom there is no returning, their sins destroyed by knowledge.

Sages look equally [7] on a Brahmin endowed with 18
knowledge and breeding, or on a cow, an elephant,
and even a dog and an outcaste.

Even here on earth, creation is conquered by 19
those whose minds are established in equality.

Brahman is spotless and is the same to all. Therefore they are established in Brahman.

One should not rejoice when obtaining the pleasant, nor be agitated when obtaining the unpleasant. Unbewildered, with firm intelligence, the knower of Brahman is established in Brahman.   20

The self who is unattached to external contacts finds happiness in the Self. Being joined by yoga to Brahman,[8] he attains imperishable happiness.   21

The enjoyments which are born of contacts (with objects) are only sources of sorrow. These have a beginning and end, O son of Kuntī; the wise man does not rejoice in them.   22

He who is able to endure here on earth, even before he is liberated from the body, the force that springs from desire and anger, he is disciplined, he is the happy man.   23

He who is happy within, whose joy is within and whose light is within; that yogin becomes Brahman and attains to the bliss of Brahman.   24

The seers whose sins are destroyed, whose dualities (doubts) are dispelled, whose selves are disciplined and who rejoice in the welfare of all beings, attain to the bliss of Brahman.   25

To these holy men who have destroyed desire and anger, who have controlled their minds, who know the Self, the bliss of Brahman is near.   26

Having excluded external contacts and having   27
fixed the sight between the eyebrows, having made
equal the incoming and outgoing breaths moving
within the nostrils;

Having controlled the senses, mind and intelli-   28
gence, the sage who has liberation [9] as his goal, who
has cast away desire, fear and anger, is freed forever.

Knowing Me as the enjoyer of sacrifices and aus-   29
terities, as the great lord of all worlds, as the friend
of all creatures, he attains peace.

*

*This is the fifth chapter, entitled "The Yoga of the Re-
nunciation of Action"* (karmasannyāsayoga) .

CHAPTER

VI

The Yoga of Meditation

The Blessed Lord said:
He who does the action that should be done with-   1
out concern for its fruits, he is a *sannyāsin,* he is
a yogin, and not he who does not light the sacred
fires and performs no rites.

Know that what they call renunciation is yoga,   2
O Pāndava, for no one becomes a yogin who has
not renounced selfish desire.

For the sage who is desirous of ascending to yoga,   3
action is called the means.[1] For the sage who has
ascended to yoga, serenity is called the means.

When one is not attached to the objects of sense   4
or to actions, and has renounced all desires,[2] then
he is said to have attained yoga.

One should lift up the self by the self, one should   5
not let the Self be degraded; for the Self alone is

the friend of the self and the Self alone is the enemy of the self.

For him who has conquered his self by the self, 6
his Self is a friend; but for him who has not conquered his self, the Self becomes hostile, like an enemy.

The highest Self of him who has conquered the 7
self and is peaceful remains ever concentrated in heat and cold, pleasure and pain, in honor and dishonor.

That yogin who is satisfied with wisdom and 8
understanding, who is unchanging and has subdued his senses, to whom a lump of clay, a rock and gold are the same is said to be disciplined.

He who is impartial to friend, companion and 9
foe, to those who are remote and neutral, to those who are hateful, to relatives, to good and evil men, excels.

Let the yogin always concentrate on the Self, 10
abiding alone in solitude, with mind and self controlled,[8] without desires and possessions.

Having set in a clean place a firm seat for himself 11
that is neither too high nor too low, made of Kusha grass, a deerskin and a cloth, one over the other;

Sitting there on the seat, making his mind one- 12
pointed, controlling the activity of his mind and

senses, let him practice yoga for the purification of the self.[4]

Holding the body, head and neck erect and mo- 13
tionless, looking steadily at the tip of his nose, not
looking in any direction,

With the self calmed and free from fear, firm in 14
the vow of celibacy, having controlled the mind,
let him sit harmonized, his thoughts on Me, ab-
sorbed in Me.

Thus always disciplining himself and with his 15
mind controlled, the yogin attains to peace, the
supreme bliss, that abides in Me.

Yoga is not for him who eats too much, or does 16
not eat at all. It is not for him, O Arjuna, who
sleeps too much or keeps too much awake.

For one who is moderate in food and amusement, 17
restrained in the performance of his actions, whose
sleep and waking are regulated, yoga destroys all
pain.

When the controlled thought is fixed on the 18
Self alone, then he who is free from all desires is
said to be disciplined.

As a lamp in a windless place does not flicker, so 19
the yogin of controlled thought, practicing yoga
of the self.

That in which thought comes to rest, curbed 20
by the practice of yoga; that in which seeing the
Self, by the self, he is content in the Self;

That in which supreme happiness, which is be- 21
yond the senses, is grasped by intelligence; that
wherein established, he knows this and does not
fall away from the truth;

That on obtaining which, he thinks no other 22
gain is greater; that wherein established, by no
sorrow, however heavy, is he moved:

Let that disconnection from union with pain 23
be known as yoga. This yoga should be practiced
with determination, with mind undismayed.

Abandoning, without exception, all the desires 24
born of egoism,⁵ restraining all the senses on every
side by the mind,

Let him come to rest, little by little, by intel- 25
ligence held firmly; and fixing the mind on the
Self, let him not think of anything else.

Whatsoever thing makes the fickle and unsteady 26
mind wander, let him restrain it and lead it back
to the control of the self alone.

This highest happiness comes to the yogin whose 27
mind is peaceful, whose passions are subdued, who
is sinless and has become one with Brahman.⁶

The yogin who thus always disciplines his self   28
and who is free from sin, easily attains the ultimate bliss of unity with Brahman.[7]

He whose self is disciplined by yoga sees the   29
Self abiding in all beings and all beings in the
Self; he sees the same in all beings.

He who sees Me everywhere and sees all in Me,   30
for him I am not lost and he is not lost for Me.

He who, established in oneness, worships Me   31
abiding in all beings, exists in Me, no matter how
otherwise he exists.

He who sees that which is pleasant or painful   32
to others is the same for himself,[8] O Arjuna, he
is considered the highest yogin.

Arjuna said:
I see no firm foundation for this yoga which is   33
declared by Thee to be (characterized by) equality,[9] O Madhusūdana, because of (man's) restless-
ness.

For the mind is indeed restless, O Krishna; it   34
is impetuous, strong and hard. I think the controlling of it is as difficult as controlling the wind.

The Blessed Lord said:
Undoubtedly, O mighty-armed one, the mind is   35
restless and hard to restrain, but by practice and
dispassion, O son of Kuntī, it can be controlled.

Yoga is hard to attain, I think, by one who is   36
not self-controlled; but for one who is self-controlled and who strives, it is possible to attain
through proper means.

Arjuna said:
He who is uncontrolled but possesses faith and   37
whose mind wanders away from yoga, not having
attained perfection in yoga, which way does he go,
O Krishna?

Fallen from both, unstable, and bewildered in   38
the path to Brahman, does he not perish like a
rent cloud, O mighty-armed one?

Thou oughtest to dispel completely this doubt   39
of mine, O Krishna, for no remover of this doubt,
other than Thee, is to be found.

The Blessed Lord said:
O Pārtha, neither in this world nor the next is   40
there any destruction of him, for no doer of the
good, dear friend, comes to an evil end.

Having attained the world of the doers of right,   41
and having dwelt there for many years, he who has
fallen from yoga is born in the house of the pure
and prosperous;

Or he may be born in the family of wise yogins;   42
for such a birth as this is harder to attain in the
world.

There he acquires the mental characteristics as-   43
sociated with his previous existence, and he strives
from that point on to perfection, O joy of the
Kurus.

By his former practice he is carried along help-   44
lessly. Even he who (merely) wishes to know of
yoga goes beyond the rules of the Veda.[10]

But the yogin who strives with perseverance,   45
who is purified of all sins and is perfected through
many lives, goes to the supreme goal.

The yogin is greater than the ascetic, he is   46
thought to be greater than even the wise; the yogin
is greater than men of ritual action; therefore, be
a yogin, O Arjuna.

And of all yogins, the one who, full of faith,   47
worships Me with his inner self abiding in Me, he
is thought by Me to be the most disciplined.

*

*This is the sixth chapter, entitled "The Yoga of Medita-
tion"* (dhyānayoga).

CHAPTER

VII

The Yoga of Wisdom
and Understanding

The Blessed Lord said:

Hear, O Pārtha, how, by attaching thy mind to   1
Me, and by practicing yoga, with reliance upon
Me, thou shalt know Me entirely, without doubt.

I will declare to thee in full this wisdom to-   2
gether with knowledge which, when known, nothing more in this world remains to be known.

Among thousands of men, perchance one strives   3
for perfection, and of those who strive and are
successful, perhaps one knows Me in essence.

This is My divided eightfold nature: earth,   4
water, fire, wind, ether, mind, intellect and self-
consciousness.[1]

This is My lower (nature). Know My other 5
higher [2] nature, O mighty-armed one, which is the
life-soul [3] by which this world is supported.

Learn that all beings arise from this (higher and 6
lower nature of Mine [4]). I am the origin of the
whole world and also its dissolution.

Nothing exists higher than Me, O winner of 7
wealth. All this (universe) is strung on Me like
jewels on a string.

I am the taste in the waters, O son of Kuntī. I 8
am the light in the moon and the sun; I am the
sacred syllable (*Om*) in all the Vedas, the sound
in ether and the manhood in men.

I am the pure fragrance in earth and the bril- 9
liance in fire; I am the life in all beings and the
austerity in ascetics.

Know Me, O Pārtha, to be the eternal seed of 10
all beings. I am the intellect of the intelligent,
the splendor of the splendid.

I am the strength of the strong which is free 11
from desire and passion. I am the desire in all
beings which is not incompatible with *dharma*,
O Lord of the Bharatas.

And of all beings that are—the harmonious 12
(*sattvic*), the passionate (*rajasic*) and even the
inert (*tamasic*)—know that these are from Me
alone. But I am not in them, they are in Me.

Deluded by these states made up of the *gunas*, 13
this whole world does not recognize Me who is
higher than these and imperishable.

This is My divine *māyā* composed of the *gunas*, 14
which is hard to pass beyond. Those who resort to
Me alone cross over this *māyā*.

The evildoers who are deluded and low among 15
men do not resort to Me. Their minds are deprived of wisdom by illusion and their nature is
demoniac.

Fourfold are the virtuous who worship Me, O 16
Arjuna: the afflicted, the wisdom seeker, the seeker
for wealth, and the wise, O Lord of the Bharatas.

Of these the wise one, who is constantly disci- 17
plined and of single-minded devotion, is the best;
extremely dear to him am I, and he is dear to Me.

All of these are noble, but the wise one I hold 18
as My very self. For he, with disciplined self, re-
sorts to Me alone as the highest goal.

At the end of many births, the man of wisdom 19
approaches Me, thinking "Vāsudeva is all." Such
a great self is difficult to find.

But those who are deprived of wisdom by their 20
desires resort to other gods, having taken up various vows, constrained by their own nature.

But whatever form a devotee with faith wishes 21
to worship, I make steady that faith of his.

Disciplined with that faith, he seeks to propi- 22
tiate that god; and he obtains his desires, for those
(the benefits) are decreed by Me.

But temporary is the fruit (obtained by) those 23
that are of small intelligence. Those who worship
the gods go to the gods; My devotees come to Me.

The foolish think of Me, the unmanifest, as hav- 24
ing (only) come into manifestation; not knowing
My higher nature which is immutable and supreme.

I am not revealed to all, being covered by My 25
power of illusion. This world is deluded and does
not recognize Me, the unborn and imperishable.

I know beings that are past, that are present and 26
that are yet to be, O Arjuna, but no one knows
Me.

All beings are born to confusion, O Bhārata, 27
and are deluded by the dualities that originate
from desire and hatred, O conqueror of the foe.

But those men of virtuous deeds whose sins are 28
ended and who are freed from the delusion of opposites worship Me with steadfast resolve.

Those who strive for liberation from old age   29
and death and have taken refuge in Me know
Brahman entirely and the supreme Self and all
action.

Those who know Me together with (My) ma-   30
terial and divine domains [5] and the highest sacrifice; they, of balanced mind, know Me even at the
time of death.

*

*This is the seventh chapter, entitled "The Yoga of Wis-
dom and Understanding"* (jñānavijñānayoga).

CHAPTER

VIII

The Yoga of
the Imperishable Brahman

Arjuna said:

What is that Brahman? What is the supreme   1
Self [1] and action, O best of beings? What is said
to be the material domain and what is declared to
be the domain of the divine?

How and what is the domain of sacrifice here in   2
this body, O Madhusūdana? How art Thou to be
known at the time of death by men of self-control?

The Blessed Lord said:

Brahman is the indestructible, the supreme; the   3
Self is called essential nature,[2] and *karma* is the
name of the creative power that causes beings to
exist.[3]

A perishable condition is the basis of all ma-   4
terial things; the spirit (*purusha*) is the basis of

77

divine elements, and I am the basis of all sacrifice here in the body, O best of embodied ones.

And whoever remembers Me alone when leav- 5
ing the body at the time of death attains to My status of being; there is no doubt of that.

Whatever state of being he remembers, upon 6
giving up his body at the end, to that he attains, O son of Kuntī; always being formed in that state.[4]

Therefore at all times think of Me and fight. 7
With mind (*manas*) and intellect (*buddhi*) set on Me, thou shalt doubtless come to Me alone.

He who is disciplined by the yoga of practice 8
and meditates on the supreme Person, his mind not straining after some other object, he reaches, O Pārtha, that supreme divine Spirit.

He who meditates on the ancient seer, the ruler, 9
who is smaller than the small, who is the supporter of all, whose form is inconceivable and who is sun-colored beyond the darkness,

At the time of death, with an unshaken mind, 10
disciplined with devotion and the strength of yoga, placing the life-force (*prāna*) between the eye-brows, he attains that supreme divine Spirit.

I shall declare to thee briefly that place which 11
the Veda-knowers call the indestructible, where as-cetics free from passion enter, and where they lead a life of chastity.[5]

He who controls the gates (of the body), con- 12
fines the mind in the heart, places the breath in
the head, establishes himself in concentration by
yoga,

Pronounces the single syllable (*Om*), which is 13
Brahman, meditates on Me as he goes forth and
abandons the body, he reaches the highest goal.

He who always thinks of Me and not of some- 14
thing else, for him, O Pārtha, who is a yogin ever
disciplined, I am easy to obtain.

Having come to Me, these great-souled men do 15
not attain rebirth, the place of sorrow and im-
permanence, for they have reached the highest
perfection.

From the world of Brahmā downwards, all 16
worlds are reborn, O Arjuna; but having come
to Me, O son of Kuntī, there is no rebirth.

They who know that the day of Brahmā is of a 17
thousand ages and that the night of Brahmā is of
a thousand ages, they are the persons who know
what day and night are.[6]

From the unmanifest, all manifestations come 18
forth at the coming of day, and at the coming of
night, they dissolve in that same thing, called the
unmanifest.

This same multitude of beings, coming forth 19
repeatedly, dissolves helplessly in the coming of

night, O Pārtha, and comes forth in the coming of day.

But higher than that unmanifest state, there is   20
another unmanifested eternal being who does not
perish when all beings perish.

This unmanifested (state) is called the Inde-   21
structible. They call that the highest goal which,
having obtained, they return not. That is My highest abode.

This is the supreme spirit, O Pārtha, obtainable   22
by unswerving devotion, in whom all beings abide
and by whom all this is pervaded.

I will declare to thee that time, O best of the   23
Bharatas, when the yogins depart and do not return
and when they depart and do return.

Fire, light, day, the lunar fortnight, the six   24
months that are the northward course (of the
sun), there the men who know Brahman go forth
to Brahman.⁷

Smoke, night, also the dark lower fortnight, the   25
six months of the southern course (of the sun),
there going forth, the yogin attains the moon's
light and returns.

These two paths, light and dark, are thought   26
to be the everlasting paths of the world. By one,
man does not return; by the other he returns
again.

Knowing these paths, O Pārtha, the yogin is not   27
perplexed. Therefore at all times be disciplined
in yoga, O Arjuna.

The yogin, having known all this, goes beyond   28
the fruits of deeds assigned in the Vedas, in sacrifices, in austerities, and in gifts, and goes to the
highest and primal place.

*

*This is the eighth chapter, entitled "The Yoga of the
Imperishable Brahman"* (aksharabrahmayoga) .

CHAPTER

IX

The Yoga of Sovereign Knowledge and Mystery

The Blessed Lord said:

I will declare to thee, who are uncomplaining, 1
this deepest secret of wisdom combined with knowledge, knowing which thou shalt be delivered from evil.

This is sovereign knowledge, a sovereign secret, 2
the highest purifier, understood immediately,[1] righteous, very easy to practice and imperishable.

Men who have no faith in this law, O oppressor 3
of the foe, do not attain Me but return to the path of ceaseless birth and rebirth.[2]

By Me, in My unmanifested form, all this world 4
is pervaded. All beings rest in Me but I do not rest in them.

And (yet) beings do not rest in Me: behold My 5
divine mystery (yoga). My Self, which is the
source of beings, sustains all beings but does not
rest in them.

Just as the great wind, blowing everywhere, 6
abides in the ether,[3] so all beings abide in Me;
know thou that.

All beings, O son of Kuntī, enter into My (ma- 7
terial) nature at the end of a world cycle, and I
send them forth again at the beginning of a new
cycle.[4]

Taking hold of My own (material) nature, I 8
send forth again and again all this multitude of
beings which are helpless, by the force of (My)
material nature.

And these actions do not bind Me, O Dhanan- 9
jaya; I am seated as one who is indifferent, unattached to these actions.

With Me as supervisor, *prakriti* sends forth all 10
moving and unmoving (things) ; by this cause, O
son of Kuntī, the world revolves.

The foolish despise Me when I assume a human 11
form, not knowing My higher nature as the great
Lord of all beings.

They abide in a fiendish and demoniac nature 12
which is deceitful; their hopes are vain, their ac-

tions are vain, their knowledge is vain, and they are devoid of mind.

But the great-souled, O Pārtha, who abide in the divine nature, worship Me with undeviating mind, knowing Me as the imperishable source of all beings. 13

Always glorifying Me and striving with steadfast resolve, and honoring Me with devotion, they worship Me ever-disciplined. 14

Others also, sacrificing with the sacrifice of wisdom, worship Me as the one, as the distinct, and as the many [5] facing in all directions. 15

I am the ritual, I am the sacrifice, I am the oblation, I am the medicinal herb, I am the sacred hymn, I am also the melted butter, I am the fire and I am the burnt offering. 16

I am the father of this world, the mother, the supporter, the grandsire, the object of knowledge, the purifier, the sacred syllable *Om,* and also the verse (*rik*), the chant (*sāma*) and the sacrificial formula (*yajus*). 17

I am the goal, upholder, lord, witness, abode, shelter and friend. I am the origin, dissolution, foundation, treasure-house and imperishable seed. 18

I give heat; I hold back and send forth the rain; I am immortality, and also death; I am being and non-being, O Arjuna. 19

The knowers of the three (Vedas) who drink 20
the Soma [6] and are purified of sin worship Me
with sacrifices and pray for the way to heaven.
Having reached the holy world of Indra, they taste
in heaven the divine enjoyments of the gods.

After enjoying the vast world of heaven,[7] they 21
return to the world of mortals when their merit is
exhausted. Thus conforming to the doctrine of the
three Vedas and desiring pleasure, they obtain the
transitory.

But to those who worship Me, thinking of no 22
other, to those who are constant in perseverance,
I bring acquisition and possession of their goal.

Even those who are devotees of other gods and 23
who worship them full of faith, even they worship
Me only, O son of Kuntī, although not according
to the prescribed rules.

For I am the recipient [8] and lord of all sacri- 24
fices. But they do not know Me in my essence and
hence they fall.

The worshipers of the gods go to the gods; the 25
worshipers of the ancestors go to the ancestors;
sacrificers of the spirits go to the spirits; and those
who sacrifice to Me come to Me.

Whoever offers Me a leaf, a flower, a fruit or 26
water with devotion, I accept that offering of devotion from the pure in heart.

Whatever thou doest, whatever thou eatest, 27
whatever thou offerest, whatever thou givest, whatever austerities thou performest, do that, O son
of Kuntī, as an offering to Me.

Thus thou shalt be freed from the bonds of ac- 28
tion which produce good and evil fruits; disciplined by the yoga of renunciation, thou shalt be
liberated and come to Me.

I am equal to all beings, there is none hateful 29
nor dear to Me. But those who worship Me with
devotion, they are in Me and I am in them.

Even if a man of very evil conduct worships 30
Me with undivided devotion, he too must be considered righteous, for he has resolved rightly.

Quickly he becomes a righteous self and obtains 31
eternal peace; O son of Kuntī, know thou that My
devotee never perishes.

They who take refuge in Me, O Pārtha, even 32
though they be born of sinful wombs,[9] women,
Vaishyās and even Shūdras, they also reach the
highest goal.

How much more, then, holy Brahmins and de- 33
voted royal sages! Having come to this perishable,
unhappy world—worship thou Me.

Fix the mind on Me, be devoted to Me, wor- 34
ship Me, salute Me; thus having disciplined the

self and having Me as the supreme goal, thou shalt
come to Me.

*

This is the ninth chapter, entitled "The Yoga of Sovereign Knowledge and Sovereign Mystery" (rājavidyārā-
jaguhyayoga).

CHAPTER

X

The Yoga of Manifestations

The Blessed Lord said:

Again, O mighty-armed one, hear My supreme word. From a desire to benefit thee, I will declare it to thee who art delighted (with it). 1

Neither the hosts of gods nor the great seers know My origin, for I am the source of the gods and the great seers in every respect. 2

He who knows Me, the unborn, the beginningless, the great Lord of the world, he among mortals is undeluded and is freed from all sins. 3

Understanding, wisdom, non-bewilderment, patience, truth, self-control, calmness, happiness, sorrow, existence, non-existence, fear and also fearlessness, 4

Non-injury,[1] equanimity, contentment, austerity, generosity, fame and ill-fame, are the different states of being which arise from Me alone. 5

The seven great seers of old and the four 6
Manus [2] are also of My nature; they were born
of My mind and from them have arisen all these
creatures in the world.

He who knows in essence this glory and power 7
of Mine is united (with Me) by unshaken discipline; there is no doubt of that.

I am the source of all; from Me all arises. 8
Knowing this, the wise worship Me, imbued with
feeling.[3]

With their thoughts fixed on Me, their lives cen- 9
tered on Me, enlightening each other and always
speaking about Me, they are content and rejoice
in Me.

To those who are always so disciplined, wor- 10
shiping Me with love, I give that yoga of intellect [4] by which they come unto Me.

Out of compassion for them, while remaining 11
in My own self-nature, I destroy the darkness born
of ignorance with the shining light of wisdom.

Arjuna said:
Thou art the supreme Brahman, the highest 12
abode, the supreme purifier, the eternal divine
spirit, the first of the gods, the unborn, the omnipresent;

So all the seers call Thee; the divine seer Nā- 13
rada, and also Asita, Devala, Vyāsa and Thyself
tellest it to me.

All this that Thou sayest to me I hold true, O 14
Keshava; neither the gods nor the demons, O
Lord, know Thy manifestation.

Only Thou knowest Thyself by Thyself, O Su- 15
preme spirit (*purushottama*), Source of beings,
Lord of creatures, God of gods, Lord of the world!

Thou shouldst tell me of Thy complete divine 16
manifestations, by which Thou pervadest these
worlds and dost abide (in them).

How may I know Thee, O Yogin, by meditat- 17
ing always? In what states of being art Thou, O
Blessed Lord, to be thought by me?

Tell me again in complete detail, O Janārdana, 18
of Thy power and manifestation. Satiety comes not
to me, hearing Thy nectarlike words.

The Blessed Lord said:
Listen, I will tell thee of My divine manifesta- 19
tions; of those which are pre-eminent, O best of
the Kurus, for there is no end to My extent.

I am the Self seated in the hearts of all beings, 20
O Gudākesha; I am the beginning, the middle,
and also the end of all beings.

Of the Ādityas [5] I am Vishnu; of the lights the   21
radiant sun; I am Marīci of the Maruts; [6] of the
stars I am the moon.

Of the Vedas I am the Sāmaveda; of the gods I   22
am Vāsava (Indra) ; of the senses I am *manas*, and
of beings I am consciousness.

And of the Rudras I am Shankara (Shiva) ; I   23
am Vittesha (Kubera) [7] of the Yakshas and Rākshasas; [8] of the Vasus I am the god of fire, and of
mountain peaks I am Meru.

Know then, O Pārtha, that of house priests I am   24
the chief, Brihaspati; of generals I am Skanda; [9]
of lakes I am the ocean.

Of the great seers I am Bhrigu; of utterances   25
the singular syllable (*Om*) ; of sacrifices the silent
sacrifice; of immovable things I am the Himālaya.

Of all trees, I am Ashvattha; [10] of divine seers   26
Nārada; of the Gandharvas [11] I am Citraratha; of
perfected beings the sage Kapila.

Know me to be Uccaihshravas [12] of horses,   27
nectar-born; Airāvata [13] of lordly elephants; and of
men the monarch.

Of weapons I am the thunderbolt; of cows I am   28
Kāmadhuk; I am the progenitor Kandarpa; [14] of
serpents I am Vāsuki.

I am Ananta of the Nāgas;[15] Varuna[16] of water   29
creatures; I am Aryama of the departed fathers,
and of guardians I am Yama.[17]

I am Prahlāda of Titans; the time of calcula-   30
tors; of wild animals I am the lion; of birds I am
Vinatā.[18]

I am the wind of purifiers; Rāma[19] of warriors;   31
of fishes I am the alligator, and of rivers I am the
Ganges.

Of creations, I am the beginning, the end and   32
also the middle, O Arjuna; of knowledge the
knowledge of the Self; I am the speech of those
who speak.

Of letters I am the letter A, and of compounds   33
the *dvandva*.[20] I am also everlasting time; I am the
Creator whose face is in every direction.

I am death, the all-devouring, and the origin of   34
all beings to come; of feminine things I am fame,
prosperity, speech, memory, intelligence, firmness
and forgiveness.

Likewise, of chants I am Brihatsāman;[21] of me-   35
ters I am Gāyatrī;[22] of months I am Mārgashīrsha;[23] and of seasons I am spring.

I am the gambling of the dishonest; the splen-   36
dor of the splendid; I am victory; I am effort; I am
the goodness of the good.

Of the Vrishnis I am Vāsudeva; of the Pāndavas 37
I am Dhanamjaya; of sages I am Vyāsa, and of poets
the poet Ushanā.

I am the rod of rulers; the policy of victory- 38
seekers; I am also the silence of secrets and the
wisdom of the wise.

And I am the seed of all beings, O Arjuna. 39
There is no being, moving or unmoving, that can
exist without Me.

There is no end to My divine manifestations, O 40
conqueror of the foe. What I have declared is
only an example of the extent of My glory.

Whatever being has glory, majesty or power, 41
know that to have originated from a portion of
My splendor.

But what is all this detailed knowledge to thee, 42
O Arjuna? I stand supporting this entire world
with only a single fraction of Myself.

*

*This is the tenth chapter, entitled "The Yoga of Mani-
festations"* (vibhūtiyoga) .

CHAPTER

XI

The Yoga of the Vision of the Universal Form

Arjuna said:
As a favor to me [1] Thou hast spoken about the 1
supreme mystery called the Self; and by Thy words
my delusion is dispelled.

The origin and dissolution of beings have been 2
heard by me in detail from Thee, O Lotus-eyed
one, and also Thy imperishable greatness.

As Thou declarest Thyself, so it is, O Supreme 3
Lord. I desire to see Thy godly form, O Purushottama!

If Thou thinkest that it can be seen by me, O 4
Lord, then reveal Thy immortal Self to me, O
Lord of Yoga!

The Blessed Lord said:
Behold, O Pārtha, My forms, by hundreds and 5

by thousands, manifold and divine, of various colors and shapes.

Behold the Ādityas, the Vasus, the Rudras, the two Ashvins, and also the Maruts. Behold, O Bhārata, many marvels not seen before. 6

Behold today the whole world, of moving and unmoving things, united in My body, O Gudākesha, and whatever else thou desirest to see. 7

But thou canst not see Me with thine own eye. I give thee a divine eye. Behold My divine yoga. 8

Sanjaya said:
Having spoken thus, O King, the great Lord of Yoga, Hari, then showed to Pārtha His supreme, divine form; 9

Of many mouths and eyes, of many marvelous visions, of many divine ornaments, of many uplifted weapons; 10

Wearing divine garlands and garments with divine perfumes and ointments, full of all wonders, radiant, infinite, His face is turned everywhere. 11

If the light of a thousand suns were to spring forth simultaneously in the sky, it would be like the light of that great Being. 12

There Pāndava beheld the whole world, divided into many parts, all united in the body of the God of gods. 13

Then filled with amazement, his hair standing 14
erect, Arjuna bowed down his head to the God
and with hands folded in salutation said:

Arjuna said:
I see all the gods in Thy body, O God, and also 15
the various kinds of beings: Brahmā, the Lord,
seated on the lotus seat, and all the sages and divine
serpents.

I see Thee, with many arms, stomachs, mouths, 16
and eyes, everywhere infinite in form; I see no end
nor middle nor beginning of Thee, O Lord of all,
O universal form!

I behold Thee with diadem, club and discus as 17
a mass of light shining everywhere with the radiance of flaming fire and the sun, difficult to regard,
beyond all measure.

Thou art the imperishable, the highest to be 18
known; Thou art the final resting place of this universe; Thou art the immortal guardian of eternal
law; Thou art, I think, the primal spirit.

I behold Thee without beginning, middle or 19
end, of infinite power, of innumerable arms, the
moon and sun as Thine eyes, Thy face as a shining
fire, burning this universe with Thy radiance.

This space between heaven and earth and all the 20
quarters of the sky is pervaded by Thee alone; seeing this Thy wondrous, terrible form, the triple
world trembles, O great one!

These hosts of gods enter Thee and some, af- 21
frighted, invoke Thee with folded hands, and hosts
of great seers and perfected ones crying "Hail!"
praise Thee with magnificent hymns.

The Rudras, the Ādityas, the Vasus, the Sādhyas, 22
the Vishvedevas, the two Ashvins, the Maruts and
the Ushmapās, and the hosts of Gandharvas, Yakshas, Asuras, and perfected ones all gaze at Thee
in amazement.

Seeing Thy great form, of many mouths and 23
eyes, O mighty-armed one, of many arms, thighs
and feet, of many bellies, of many terrible tusks,
the worlds tremble, and so do I.

Seeing Thee touching the sky and blazing with 24
many colors, with opened mouths and shining
enormous eyes, my inmost self is shaken and I find
no strength nor peace, O Vishnu!

Seeing Thy mouths, terrible with tusks, like 25
time's devouring fire, I know not the directions
of the sky and I find no security. Have mercy, O
Lord of gods, Abode of the world!

And these sons of Dhritarāshtra, all of them, to- 26
gether with the hosts of kings, Bhīshma, Drona,
and also Karna, together with our chief warriors

Are rushing into Thy mouths, dreadful with ter- 27
rible tusks. Some are seen with pulverized heads,
stuck between Thy teeth.

As the many water currents of rivers race head- 28
long to the ocean, so these heroes of the world of
men enter into Thy flaming mouths.

As moths swiftly enter a blazing fire and perish 29
there, so these creatures swiftly enter Thy mouths
and perish.

Swallowing all the worlds from every side, Thou 30
lickest them up with Thy flaming mouths; Thy
fierce rays fill the whole world with radiance and
scorch it, O Vishnu!

Tell me who Thou art with so terrible a form! 31
Salutation to Thee, O best of gods, be merciful!
I wish to know Thee, the primal one; for I do
not understand Thy ways.

The Blessed Lord said:
Time[2] am I, the world destroyer, matured, 32
come forth to subdue the worlds here. Even without thee, all the warriors arrayed in the opposing
armies shall cease to be.

Therefore stand up and win fame. Conquering 33
thy enemies, enjoy a prosperous kingdom. By Me
they have already been slain. Be thou the mere
instrument, O Savyasācin.

Slay thou Drona, Bhīshma, Jayadratha, Karna, 34
and the other warrior-heroes too, who have already been slain by Me. Be not distressed, fight!
Thou shalt conquer thy enemies in battle.

Sanjaya said:
Having heard this utterance of Keshava   35
(Krishna), Kirīttī (Arjuna), trembling and with
folded hands, saluted Him again, and bowing down
fearfully said to Krishna in a faltering voice,

Arjuna said:
It is right, O Hrishīkesha, that the world re-   36
joices and is pleased by Thy fame. Ogres flee in
terror in all directions, and all the hosts of perfected ones bow down before Thee.

And why should they not prostrate themselves,   37
O Great One, who art greater than Brahmā, the
primal creator? O infinite one! Lord of the gods!
O refuge of the worlds! Thou art the imperishable; Thou are being and non-being, and that
which is beyond both.

Thou art the first of the gods, the primal spirit;   38
Thou art the highest treasure-house of this world;
Thou art the knower and that which is to be
known, and the highest goal. By Thee this universe is pervaded, O Thou of infinite form!

Thou art Vāyu [3] and Yama, Agni,[4] Varuna, Sha-   39
shānka,[5] and Prajāpati, the grandsire. Hail, hail
to Thee a thousand times; hail, hail to Thee again
and also again!

Hail to Thee in front and in the rear, hail to   40
Thee on every side, O all; infinite in power and
immeasurable in strength. Thou penetratest all
and therefore Thou art all.

For whatever I said in rashness from negligence   41
or even from affection thinking Thou art my
friend, and not knowing Thy greatness, calling
Thee "O Krishna, O Yādava, O comrade,"

And whatever disrespect I showed Thee for the   42
sake of jesting, whether at play, on the bed, seated
or at meals, whether alone or in the company of
others, O sinless one, I pray forgiveness from
Thee, the boundless one.

Thou art the father of this moving and unmov-   43
ing world. Thou art the object of its reverence and
its greatest teacher. There is nothing equal to
Thee, how then could anyone in the triple-world
surpass Thee, O Thou of incomparable power!

Therefore, bending down and prostrating my   44
body, I ask Thy grace; Thou, O Lord, shouldst
bear with me as a father to his son, as friend with
friend, as a lover to his beloved.

Having seen what was never seen before, I am   45
glad, but my mind is distraught with fear. Show
me, O Lord, that other form of Thine; O Lord of
gods, be gracious, O refuge of the world.

I wish to see Thee as before with Thy crown,   46
mace and disk in hand. Be that four-armed form,
O thousand-armed one of universal form!

The Blessed Lord said:
By My grace, O Arjuna, and through My great   47
power, was shown to thee this highest form, full of

splendor, universal, infinite, primal, which no one but thee has seen before.

Not by the Vedas, by sacrifices or study, not by gifts, nor ritual, nor severe austerities can I, in such a form, be seen in the world of men by any other but thee, O hero of the Kurus.   48

Be not afraid nor bewildered in seeing this terrible form of Mine. Without fear and of satisfied mind, behold again My other form.   49

Sanjaya said:
Having thus spoken to Arjuna, Vāsudeva revealed again His own form. The great one, having become again the gracious form, comforted him in his fear.   50

Arjuna said:
Seeing again this Thy gracious human form, O Janārdana, I have become composed of mind and restored to my normal nature.   51

The Blessed Lord said:
This form of Mine, which is very difficult to see, thou hast seen. Even the gods are constantly desiring the sight of this form.   52

In the form that thou hast seen Me, I cannot be seen by the Vedas, by austerity, by gift or sacrifice.   53

But by devotion to Me alone can I in this form, O Arjuna, be known and seen in essence, and entered into, O oppressor of the foe.   54

He who does My work, who regards Me as his 55
goal, who is devoted to Me, who is free from attachment and is free from enmity to all beings, he
comes to Me, O Pāndava.

*

*This is the eleventh chapter, entitled "The Yoga of the
Vision of the Universal Form"* (vishvarūpadarshana-
yoga) .

CHAPTER

XII

The Yoga of Devotion

Arjuna said:

Those devotees who are always disciplined and honor Thee, and those who worship the Imperishable and the Unmanifest—which of these are more learned in yoga? 1

The Blessed Lord said:

Those who, fixing their mind on Me, worship Me with complete discipline and with supreme faith, them I consider to be the most learned in yoga. 2

But those who worship the Imperishable, the Undefinable, the Unmanifested, the Omnipresent, the Unthinkable, the Immovable, the Unchanging, the Constant, 3

And have restrained all their senses, and are equal-minded and rejoice in the welfare of all beings—they also obtain Me. 4

The difficulty of those whose minds are fixed on 5
the Unmanifested is much greater; the goal of
the Unmanifested is hard for the embodied to attain.

But those who renounce all actions in Me and 6
are intent on Me,[1] who worship Me with complete
discipline and meditate on Me,

These, whose thoughts are fixed on Me, I quickly 7
lift up from the ocean of death and rebirth, O
Pārtha.

Place thy mind on Me alone, make thy intellect 8
enter into Me, and thou shalt dwell in Me hereafter. Of this there is no doubt.

But if thou art not able to fix thy thought firmly 9
on Me, then seek to obtain Me by the yoga of practice,[2] O Dhananjaya.

If thou art incapable even of practice, then be 10
devoted to My service; performing actions for My
sake, thou shalt obtain perfection.

If thou art unable to do even this, then, with 11
thy self controlled, resort to My yoga and renounce
the fruit of all action.

Better indeed is knowledge than practice; and 12
better than knowledge is meditation; better than
meditation is the renunciation of the fruit of action,
for from renunciation peace immediately comes.

He who has no ill feeling to any being, who is 13
friendly and compassionate, without selfishness and
egoism, who is the same in pain and pleasure and is
patient,

The yogin who is thus always content, self- 14
controlled and of firm resolve, and whose mind and
intellect are given over to Me; he is My devotee and
is dear to Me.

He before whom the world is not afraid and who 15
is not afraid before the world, and who is free from
joy and impatience, fear and agitation, he is dear
to Me.

He who is disinterested, pure, skillful, uncon- 16
cerned and controlled, who has abandoned all undertakings, he, My devotee, is dear to Me.

He who neither rejoices nor hates, neither 17
grieves nor desires, who has renounced good and
evil and who is devoted, he is dear to Me.

He who is alike to enemy and friend, also to 18
honor and disgrace, who is alike to cold and heat,
pleasure and pain, and is freed from attachment,

He who is thus indifferent to blame and praise, 19
who is silent and is content with anything, who is
homeless,[3] of steady mind and is devoted—that
man is dear to Me.

But those who have faith and are intent on Me 20
and who follow this nectar of righteousness which

has been declared by Me—those devotees are exceedingly dear to Me.

＊

This is the twelfth chapter, entitled "The Yoga of Devotion" (bhaktiyoga) .

CHAPTER

XIII

The Yoga of the Distinction Between the Field and the Knower of the Field

The Blessed Lord said:

This body,[1] O son of Kuntī, is called the field,[2] 1
and he who knows this is called the knower of the
field [3] by those who know him.

Know Me as the Knower of the field in all fields, 2
O Bhārata; the knowledge of the field and the
knower of the field, this I hold to be (real) knowledge.

Hear from Me briefly what the field is, what its 3
nature is, what its modifications are, whence it
comes, who he (the knower of the field) is and
what his powers are.

This has been sung by the seers in many ways; 4
in various hymns distinctly and also in the well-

reasoned and definite words of the aphorisms about Brahman.[4]

The gross elements, the I-sense, the intellect and 5
also the unmanifested, the ten senses and one (the
mind) and the five objects of the senses; [5]

Desire, hatred, pleasure, pain, the organism, in- 6
telligence and firmness; this, briefly described, is
the field together with its modifications.

Absence of pride and deceit, non-violence, pa- 7
tience, uprightness, service of a teacher, purity,
steadfastness, self-control;

Indifference to the objects of sense, lack of ego 8
and a perception of the evil [6] of birth, death, old
age, sickness and pain;

Non-attachment, absence of clinging to son, wife, 9
home and the like; a constant equal-mindedness to
desirable and undesirable occurrences;

Single-minded yoga and unswerving devotion to 10
Me, cultivation of lonely places, dislike for a crowd
of people;

Constancy in the knowledge of the Self, insight 11
into the end of essential knowledge [7]—this is declared to be knowledge: ignorance is what is other
than that.

I will declare that which is to be known, by 12
knowing which one gains immortality. It is the

beginningless supreme Brahman who is called neither being nor non-being.

With his hands and feet everywhere, with eyes,   13
heads and mouths on all sides, with his ears everywhere; he dwells in the world, enveloping all.

Appearing [8] to have the qualities of all the senses,   14
and yet free from all the senses; unattached and yet
supporting all; free from the *gunas* and yet enjoying the *gunas*,

It is outside and within all beings. It is unmoving   15
and moving. It is too subtle to be known. It is far
away and it is also near.

It is undivided and yet seems to be divided in all   16
beings. It is to be known as supporting all beings
and as absorbing and creating them.

It is also, it is said, the light of lights beyond   17
darkness; it is knowledge, the object of knowledge,
and the goal of knowledge; it is seated in the hearts
of all.

Thus the field, and also knowledge and the   18
object of knowledge, have been briefly declared.
Understanding this, My devotee becomes fit for
My state of being.

Know that both *prakriti* and *purusha* are begin-   19
ningless; and know also that modifications and the
gunas are born of *prakriti*.

Prakriti is said to be the cause of the generation 20
of causes and agents, and *purusha* is said to be the
cause of the experience of pleasure and pain.[9]

The *purusha* abiding in *prakriti* experiences the 21
gunas born of *prakriti*. Attachment to the *gunas* is
the cause of his births in good and evil wombs.

The highest spirit in this body is said to be the 22
witness,[10] the consenter,[11] the supporter,[12] the experiencer,[13] the great Lord, the supreme Self.

He who knows the *purusha* and *prakriti* together 23
with its *gunas,* though in whatever state he may
exist, he is not born again.

Some by meditation see the Self in the self by 24
the self; others by the yoga of discrimination, and
still others by the yoga of action.

Yet others, not knowing this but hearing it from 25
others, honor it, and they too cross beyond death
through their devotion to the scripture which they
have heard.

Whatever being is born, immovable or moving, 26
know, O best of the Bharatas, that it (arises) from
the union of the field and the knower of the field.

He who sees the supreme Lord abiding equally 27
in all beings, not perishing when they perish, he
(truly) sees.

Seeing the same Lord established equally every- 28
where, he does not harm the Self by the self, and
he then attains the highest goal.

He who sees that actions are performed only by 29
prakriti and likewise that the self is not the doer,
he truly sees.

When he perceives the various states of being 30
abiding in the One and extending from it, then
he attains Brahman.

Because this imperishable supreme Self is begin- 31
ningless and without attributes, though it abides
in the body, O son of Kuntī, it neither acts nor is
affected (by actions).

As the omnipresent ether, because of its subtlety, 32
is not affected, so the Self, abiding in every body,
is not affected.

As the one sun illumines this whole world, O 33
Bhārata, so does the owner of this field illumine
the whole field.

They who thus know, by the eye of knowledge, 34
the distinction between the field and the knower of
the field, and the freedom of beings from *prakriti,*
they attain to the Supreme.

*

*This is the thirteenth chapter, entitled "The Yoga of
the Distinction Between the Field and the Knower of
the Field"* (kshetrakshetrajñavibhāgayoga).

CHAPTER

XIV

The Yoga of the Distinction of the Three Gunas

The Blessed Lord said:

I will declare again that highest wisdom, the best 1
of all wisdom, knowing which all the sages have departed from this world to the highest perfection.

Having resorted to this wisdom and become like 2
My state of being, they are not born even at the time of world creation nor are they disturbed at the time of dissolution.

My womb is the great Brahman; in that I place 3
the seed, and the birth of all beings comes from that, O Bhārata.

Whatever forms are born in all wombs, O son of 4
Kuntī, the great Brahman is their womb and I am the father that gives the seed.

Sattva, rajas, and *tamas,* the *gunas* born of *pra-kriti,* bind the imperishable embodied (soul) in the body, O mighty-armed one.

Of these, *sattva,* because of its stainlessness, is   6
illuminating and healthy. It binds by attachment to happiness and by attachment to knowledge,[1] O sinless one.

Know that *rajas* is of the nature of desire whose   7
source is thirst and attachment. It, O son of Kuntī, binds the embodied (soul) by attachment to actions.

Know that *tamas* is born of ignorance, the de-   8
luder of all embodied beings. It binds, O Bhārata, by carelessness, indolence and sleep.

Sattva attaches one to happiness, *rajas* to action,   9
O Bhārata, and *tamas,* obscuring wisdom, attaches one to carelessness.

When *sattva* overpowers *rajas* and *tamas,* it pre-   10
vails, O Bhārata. When *rajas* overpowers *sattva* and *tamas,* it prevails, and likewise when *tamas* over-powers *sattva* and *rajas,* it prevails.

When the light of knowledge appears in all the   11
gates of this body, then one may know that *sattva* has increased.

Greed, activity, the undertaking of actions, rest-   12
lessness and longing, these are produced when *rajas* has increased, O best of the Bharatas.

Darkness, inactivity, negligence and delusion, 13
these are produced when *tamas* has increased, O joy
of the Kurus.

When *sattva* has increased and the embodied one 14
dies, he then attains the pure worlds of those who
know the highest.

Meeting death when *rajas* prevails, he is born 15
among those attached to action; and meeting death
when *tamas* prevails, he is born in the wombs of
the deluded.

The fruit of action well done, they say, is *sattvic* 16
and pure; while the fruit of *rajas* is pain, and the
fruit of *tamas* is ignorance.

From *sattva* knowledge is born, from *rajas* greed, 17
and from *tamas* arises negligence and delusion and
also ignorance.

Those who abide in *sattva* rise upward; the *ra-* 18
jasic stay in the middle, and the *tamasic,* abiding in
the lower activities of the modes,[2] sink down.

When the seer perceives no doer other than the 19
gunas and knows that which is higher than the
gunas, he attains to My being.

When the embodied soul transcends these three 20
gunas, whose origin is in the body,[3] it is freed from

birth, death, old age and pain, and attains immortality.

Arjuna said:
What are the marks of one who has transcended 21
the three *gunas,* O Lord? What is his conduct? How
does he go beyond these three *gunas?*

The Blessed Lord said:
He does not abhor illumination, activity or de- 22
lusion when they arise, O Pāndava, nor desire them
when they cease.

He who is seated like one indifferent and undis- 23
turbed by the *gunas,* who thinks "the *gunas* alone
act," who stands apart and remains firm,

To whom pleasure and pain are alike, who 24
abides in the self, to whom a lump of clay, a rock,
and gold are the same, to whom the pleasant and
unpleasant are equal, who is firm, to whom blame
and praise of himself are the same;

To whom honor and dishonor are the same, to 25
whom the parties of friends and enemies are the
same, who has abandoned all undertakings—he is
called the man who transcends the *gunas.*

He who serves Me with unswerving *bhakti yoga,* 26
having transcended these *gunas,* is fit to become
Brahman.

For I am the abode of Brahman, of the immortal   27
and imperishable, of eternal righteousness and of
absolute bliss.

*

*This is the fourteenth chapter, entitled "The Yoga of
the Distinction of the Three Gunas"* (gunatrayavibhāga-
yoga) .

CHAPTER

XV

The Yoga of the Highest Spirit

The Blessed Lord said:

With its roots above and its branches below (so) 1
ιey speak of the imperishable peepal tree. Its
leaves are the Vedic hymns and he who knows this
is a knower of the Veda.

Its branches spread below and above, nourished 2
by the *gunas,* with the objects of sense as its sprouts,
and below in the world of men stretch the roots that
result in actions.

Its form is thus not comprehended here, nor its 3
end nor its beginning nor its foundation. Cutting
this firmly rooted tree with the strong weapon of
non-attachment;

Then that path must be sought from which, 4
having gone, men no longer return (thinking), "I

seek refuge in that primal spirit from which issued forth this ancient cosmic activity."

Those who are without pride or delusion, who have conquered the evil of attachment, who are established in the inner self, their desires departed, who are freed from the pairs known as pleasure and pain and who are undeluded, go to that imperishable place.   5

The sun does not illumine it, nor the moon nor fire. That is My highest abode; after men go there, they never return.   6

A portion of Me in the world of the living becomes a living soul,[1] eternal, and draws along the (five) senses and the mind as sixth, that rest in *prakriti.*   7

When the Lord acquires a body and also when He departs from it, He goes, taking these along, as the wind carries fragrances from their home.   8

He enjoys the objects of the senses, making use of the ear, the eye, touch, taste and smell, and also the mind.   9

The deluded do not perceive Him when He departs or when He stays, when He experiences objects while accompanied by the *gunas;* those who have the eye of wisdom see Him.   10

The yogins who strive also see Him established 11
in their Self; but the mindless, whose self is unper-
fected, although striving, do not see Him.

That splendor which issues from the sun and il- 12
lumines the whole world; that which is in the moon
and that which is in the fire, know that splendor as
Mine.

Entering the earth, I support all beings by My 13
power; and becoming the sapful Soma, I nourish all
plants.

And becoming the fire of life dwelling in the 14
bodies of living beings and united with the life-
breaths, I cook (digest) the four kinds of food.

I am seated in the hearts of all; from Me (come) 15
memory,[2] wisdom and argument.[3] I am that which
is to be known by the Vedas; I am the author of the
Vedānta (*Upanishads*), and I am also the knower
of the Vedas.

There are two spirits in this world: the perish- 16
able and the imperishable. The perishable is all
beings and the imperishable is called Kūtastha (the
unchanging).

But there is another, the highest Spirit (*purushottama*) called the supreme Self,[4] who, as the imperishable Lord, enters into the three worlds and
sustains them.

Since I transcend the perishable and am higher   18
even than the imperishable, I am renowned in the
world and in the Vedas as the highest Spirit.

He who undeluded thus knows Me as the highest   19
Spirit is the knower of all; he worships Me with his
whole being, O Bhārata.

Thus the most secret doctrine has been spoken   20
by Me, O sinless one. Being enlightened about this,
one will have (true) enlightenment and will have
done his work, O Bhārata.

*

*This is the fifteenth chapter, entitled "The Yoga of the
Highest Spirit"* (purushottamayoga) .

CHAPTER

XVI

The Yoga of the Distinction Between the Divine and Demoniac Endowments

The Blessed Lord said:

Fearlessness, purity of being, steadfastness in the   1
yoga of wisdom, charity, self-control and sacrifice,
study of the Veda, austerity, uprightness;

Non-violence, truth, absence of anger, renuncia-   2
tion, peace, absence of guile, compassion towards
beings, absence of covetousness, gentleness, mod-
esty, absence of fickleness;

Majesty, forgiveness, fortitude, purity, absence of   3
malice and excessive pride—these are the endowments of one who is born with the divine nature, O
Bhārata.

Hypocrisy, arrogance, excessive pride and anger,   4
harshness and also ignorance—these are the endow-

ments of one who is born with the demoniac nature,
O Pārtha.

The divine endowments are said to lead to lib- 5
eration; the demoniac to bondage. Do not grieve,
O Pāndava, thou art born with divine endowments.

There are two kinds of beings created in this 6
world, the divine and the demoniac. The divine has
been described in detail. Hear from me, O Pārtha,
of the demoniac.

Demoniac men do not know about activity or its 7
cessation. Neither purity nor right conduct nor
truth is in them.

They say that the world is without truth, with- 8
out a moral basis, without a God, that it is not originated by regular causation, but that it is caused by
desire.[1]

Holding fast to this view, these lost souls of little 9
intelligence and of cruel deeds come forth as enemies for the destruction of the world.

Attaching themselves to insatiable desire, filled 10
with hypocrisy, pride and arrogance, holding false
views through delusion, they act with impure motives.

Surrendering themselves to innumerable cares 11
which end only with death, making the enjoyment
of desires their highest aim, convinced that this is
all;

Bound by hundreds of ties of desire, devoted to 12
lust and anger, they strive for accumulated wealth,
by unjust means, for the satisfaction of their desires.

"This I have won today; this desire I shall at- 13
tain; this is mine and this wealth shall also be
mine."

"I have slain this enemy, and I shall slay others 14
also. I am the lord, the enjoyer; I am perfect,
strong and happy,"

"I am wealthy and well-born. Who else is there 15
like me? I shall sacrifice, I shall give, I shall rejoice"
—thus speak those who are deluded by ignorance.

Bewildered by many fancies, enveloped by the 16
net of delusions and addicted to the satisfaction of
desires, they fall into an impure hell.

Self-conceited, stubborn, filled with pride and 17
arrogance of wealth, they worship by performing
sacrifices in name only, hypocritically, and against
all the prescribed rules.

Possessed of egotism, force, pride, desire and an- 18
ger, these envious ones hate Me in the bodies of
themselves and others.

These cruel and hateful low men, these wicked 19
ones, I constantly throw back into the cycle of existence, into demoniac wombs.

Having fallen into demoniac wombs, these de- 20
luded ones, from birth to death, do not attain Me,
O son of Kuntī; they go to the lowest place.

This is the threefold gate of hell which leads to 21
the ruin of the soul: desire, anger and greed; therefore one should abandon these three.

Freed from these three gates of darkness, O son 22
of Kuntī, a man does what is good for his self and
then attains the highest goal.

He who neglects the laws of the scripture and 23
acts according to the promptings of his desire does
not attain perfection, nor happiness, nor the highest goal.

Therefore let the scripture [2] be thy authority in 24
determining what should and should not be done.
Knowing what is declared by the rules of the scripture, thou shouldst do action in this world.

*

*This is the sixteenth chapter, entitled "The Yoga of the
Distinction Between the Divine and Demoniac Endowments"* (daivāsurasanpadvibhāgayoga) .

CHAPTER

XVII

The Yoga of the Threefold Division of Faith

Arjuna said:

What is the state of those who, (though) neglecting the laws of scripture, perform sacrifices filled with faith, O Krishna? Is it one of *sattva, rajas* or *tamas?*   1

The Blessed Lord said:

The faith of the embodied, which is born from their nature, is threefold: it is *sattvic, rajasic,* and *tamasic.* Hear about it now.   2

The faith of every man is in accord with his innate nature,[1] O Bhārata. Man is made up of faith. Whatever faith a man has, that he is.   3

Sattvic men worship the gods, *rajasic* men worship demigods and demons, and others, *tamasic* men, worship elemental spirits and ghosts.   4

Those men who, impelled by hypocrisy and ego- 5
tism and filled with desire, passion and violence,
perform cruel austerities which are not enjoined
by the scriptures,

Who starve the group of elements within the 6
body and even Me dwelling in the body—know
that these fools are demoniac in their resolves.

And the food which is dear to all men is of three 7
kinds, as are also their sacrifice, austerity and charity. Hear now the distinction between them.

The foods which increase life, energy, strength, 8
health, happiness and cheerfulness, which are tasty,
rich, substantial and agreeable, are dear to the man
of *sattva*.

The foods that are bitter, sour, salty, very hot, 9
pungent, dry and burning, which produce pain,
grief and sickness, are desired by the man of *rajas*.

That which is spoiled, tasteless, putrid, stale, left- 10
over and unclean is the food dear to the man of
tamas.

The sacrifice which is offered according to the 11
scriptures by those who are not desirous of reward
and who hold firmly to the idea that it ought to be
performed is *sattvic*.

That which is offered with a view to reward and 12
for the sake of display, O best of the Bhāratas, know
that sacrifice to be *rajasic*.

The sacrifice which is not in conformity with the   13
scriptures, in which food is not given, in which
hymns are not recited nor fees paid, and which is
devoid of faith, they declare to be *tamasic.*

(Paying) homage to the gods, to the twice-born,   14
to teachers and the wise; (practicing) purity, uprightness, chastity, non-violence, this is called the
austerity of the body.

(Speaking) words that cause no excitement, but   15
are truthful, pleasant and beneficial; and the practice of (Vedic) study—this is called the austerity
of speech.

(Attaining) tranquillity of mind, gentleness, si-   16
lence, self-control, purity of being—this is called
the austerity of mind.

This threefold austerity performed with the   17
highest faith by men who are disciplined and who
are not desirous of reward they call *sattvic.*

That austerity which is performed hypocritically   18
for the sake of respect, honor and reverence is said
to be *rajasic;* it is unstable and impermanent.

That austerity which is performed with foolish   19
stubbornness or with self-torture, or for the sake of
destroying another, is declared to be *tamasic.*

That gift which is given to one from whom no   20
return is anticipated, simply because it ought to be

given, and which is given to a worthy person in the proper place and time, that gift is thought to be *sattvic*.

But that gift which is given for the sake of a 21 return favor or with a view to reward or which is painful to give is said to be *rajasic*.

And that gift which is given at an improper place 22 and time to an unworthy person, without respect and with contempt, that is declared to be *tamasic*.

"*Om, Tat, Sat*"—this is recorded as the threefold 23 designation of Brahman. By this the Brahmins, the Vedas and the sacrifices were ordained of old.

Therefore, upon the pronouncing of "*Om*," the 24 acts of sacrifice, gift and austerity enjoined in the scripture are always undertaken by the knowers of Brahman.[2]

And with "*Tat*" the acts of sacrifice and austerity 25 and the various acts of giving are performed by those desirous of liberation, without aiming at reward.

"*Sat*" is employed in the sense of "the real" and 26 "the good," and so also the word "*Sat*" is used for praiseworthy action, O Pārtha.

Steadfastness in sacrifice, austerity and gift is also 27 called "*Sat*," and action for the sake of these is also called "*Sat*."

Whatever offering or gift is made, whatever aus- 28
terity or act is practiced without faith is called
"asat," O Pārtha; it is naught here and hereafter.

*

*This is the seventeenth chapter, entitled "The Yoga of
the Threefold Division of Faith"* (shraddhātrayavibhā-
gayoga) .

CHAPTER

XVIII

The Yoga of Freedom by Renunciation

Arjuna said:
I desire to know, O mighty-armed one, the true   1
essence of renunciation and of abandonment, O
Hrishikesha, and the distinction between them, O
Keshimishūdana.

The Blessed Lord said:
Sages know "renunciation" as the giving up of   2
acts of desire; the surrendering of the fruits of all
actions the wise call "abandonment."

Some wise men say that action should be aban-   3
doned as evil; others that acts of sacrifice, gift and
austerity should not be abandoned.

Hear now, O best of the Bharatas, My conclusion   4
about abandonment: abandonment, O tiger among
men, is explained to be threefold.

Acts of sacrifice, gift and austerity ought not to be abandoned, rather they should be performed; for sacrifice, gift and austerity are purifiers of the wise. 5

These actions ought to be performed, abandoning attachment and fruits, O Pārtha; this is My decided and highest judgment. 6

The renunciation of an action that is prescribed (by scripture) is not proper. The abandonment of that, because of delusion, is said to be of the nature of *tamas*. 7

He who abandons an action because it is painful or from fear of physical pain performs a *rajasic* kind of abandonment: he does not obtain the fruit of abandonment. 8

He who performs a prescribed action because it ought to be done, abandoning attachment and the fruit, that abandonment, O Arjuna, is thought to be *sattvic*. 9

The wise man, the abandoner, whose doubts are removed, who is filled with goodness, does not hate unpleasant action and is not attached to pleasant action. 10

It is impossible for an embodied being to abandon actions entirely; he who abandons the fruit of action is called the (true) abandoner. 11

Undesired, desired, and mixed: threefold is the 12
fruit of action for the non-abandoner in the hereafter. But there is none whatever for the renouncer.

Learn from Me, O mighty-armed, these five 13
causes, as declared in the Sānkhya, for the accomplishment of all action.

The body, the agent, the instruments of various 14
kinds, the various activities, and destiny,[1] as the
fifth:

Whatever action a man undertakes with body, 15
speech or mind, whether it be right or wrong, these
are its five causes.

That being so, he who, because of his untrained 16
intelligence, sees himself as the sole actor is a fool,
and does not see.

He who is not egoistic, whose intelligence is not 17
affected, though he slay these people, he slays not
nor is he bound.

Knowledge, the object of knowledge, and the 18
knower are the threefold incentives to action; the
instrument, the action, and the actor are the threefold constituents of action.

Knowledge, action, and the actor are said, in the 19
theory of the *gunas,* to be of just three kinds, according to the distinction of *gunas.* Hear of these
also.

That knowledge by which the one imperish- 20
able Being is seen in all beings, undivided in the
divided, know that knowledge to be *sattvic*.

That knowledge which sees various beings of 21
different kinds in all beings, because of their sepa-
rateness, know that knowledge is *rajasic*.

But that which is attached to one effect as if it 22
were the whole, without reason, without grasping
the essential, and insignificant, is declared to be
tamasic.

An action which is obligatory, which is per- 23
formed free from attachment and without desire
or hate by one who is undesirous of its fruit, is said
to be *sattvic*.

But action which is done with great exertion by 24
one who seeks to fulfill his desires or by one who
is selfish is called *rajasic*.

That action which is undertaken without re- 25
gard to consequence, to loss and injury, and to
one's own capacity, through delusion, is called
tamasic.

The actor who is free from attachment, who is 26
not egotistic,[2] who is full of firmness and con-
fidence, who is unchanged in success or failure, is
called *sattvic*.

The actor who is passionate, who is desirous of 27
the fruit of action, who is greedy, of harmful na-

ture, who is impure and full of joy and sorrow, is called *rajasic.*

The actor who is undisciplined, vulgar, stubborn, deceitful, malicious, lazy, despondent and procrastinating is said to be *tamasic.*   28

Hear now about the threefold distinction of intelligence and also of firmness, according to the *gunas,* to be set forth fully and separately, O Dhananjaya.   29

That which knows activity and inactivity, what ought to be done and what ought not to be done, what is to be feared and what is not to be feared, bondage and liberation, that intelligence, O Pārtha, is *sattvic.*   30

That by which one understands incorrectly right and wrong, what ought to be done and what ought not to be done, that intelligence, O Pārtha, is *rajasic.*   31

That which, covered by darkness, thinks what is wrong is right, and sees all things as perverted, that intelligence, O Pārtha, is *tamasic.*   32

That firmness by which one holds the activities of the mind, the life-breaths and the senses, by unwavering yoga, that, O Pārtha, is *sattvic.*   33

That firmness by which one holds to duty, pleasure and wealth, O Arjuna, with attachment and desirous of the fruits, that, O Pārtha, is *rajasic.*   34

That firmness by which the fool does not aban- 35
don sleep, fear, grief, depression and pride, that, O
Pārtha, is *tamasic*.

Hear now from me the threefold happiness, O 36
best of the Bharatas, in which man rejoices by long
practice and comes to the end of his suffering.

That which is like poison in the beginning and 37
like nectar in the end, which is born from the serenity of self and intellect, that happiness is called
sattvic.

That which (arises) from the union of the senses 38
and their objects and which is like nectar in the beginning and poison in the end, that happiness is
recorded as *rajasic*.

That which deludes the self in the beginning and 39
in the end and which arises from sleep, sloth and
carelessness, that happiness is declared to be *tamasic*.

There is no thing on earth or in heaven or even 40
among the gods who is free from these three
gunas born of *prakriti*.

The actions of Brahmins, Kshtriyas and Vaishyas, 41
and of Shūdras, O conqueror of the foe, are distinguished according to the *gunas* that arise from their
innate nature.

Calmness, self-control, austerity, purity, pa- 42
tience, uprightness, wisdom, knowledge and reli-

gious belief are the actions of the Brahmin, born
of his nature.

Heroism, majesty, firmness, skill and not fleeing   43
in battle, generosity and lordship, are the actions
of the Kshatriya, born of his nature.

Agriculture, cattle-tending and trade are the ac-   44
tions of a Vaishya, born of his nature; action whose
character is service is likewise that of the Shūdra,
born of his nature.

A man obtains perfection by being devoted to   45
his own proper action. Hear then how one who is
intent on his own action finds perfection.

By worshiping him, from whom all beings arise   46
and by whom all this is pervaded, through his own
proper action, a man attains perfection.

Better is one's own *dharma*, though imperfect,   47
than the *dharma* of another, well performed. One
does not incur sin when doing the action prescribed
by one's own nature.

One should not abandon his natural-born action,   48
O son of Kuntī, even if it be faulty, for all undertakings are clouded with faults as fire by smoke.

He whose intelligence is unattached everywhere,   49
whose self is conquered, who is free from desire, he
obtains, through renunciation, the supreme perfection of actionlessness.

Learn from me, briefly, O son of Kuntī, how he 50
who has attained perfection also attains to Brahman, the highest state of wisdom.

Disciplined with a pure intelligence, firmly con- 51
trolling oneself, abandoning sound and other sense-
objects and throwing aside passion and hatred;

Dwelling in solitude, eating little, controlling 52
speech, body and mind, constantly engaged in the
yoga of meditation[8] and taking refuge in dispassion;

Freed from egotism, force, arrogance, desire, 53
anger and possession; unselfish, peaceful—he is fit
to become Brahman.

Having become Brahman, tranquil in the Self, 54
he neither grieves nor desires. Regarding all beings
as equal, he attains supreme devotion to Me.

By devotion he knows Me, what my measure is 55
and what I am essentially; then, having known Me
essentially, he enters forthwith into Me.

Ever performing all actions, taking refuge in 56
Me, he obtains by My grace the eternal, imperishable abode.

Renouncing with thy thought all actions to Me, 57
intent on Me, taking refuge in the yoga of intellect,
fix thy mind constantly on Me.

If thy mind is on Me, thou shalt, by My grace, 58
cross over all obstacles; but if, from egotism, thou
wilt not listen, thou shalt perish.

If, centered in egotism, thou thinkest "I will not 59
fight," vain is this thy resolution; *prakriti* will com-
pel thee.

That which thou wishest not to do, through de- 60
lusion, O son of Kuntī, that thou shalt do helplessly,
bound by thine own action born of thy nature.

The Lord abides in the hearts of all beings, O 61
Arjuna, causing all beings to revolve by His power
(*māyā*), as if they were mounted on a machine.

Go to Him alone for shelter with all thy being, 62
O Bhārata. By His grace, thou shalt obtain supreme
peace and the eternal abode.

Thus the wisdom, more secret than all secrets, 63
has been declared to thee by Me. Having considered it fully, do as thou choosest.

Hear again My supreme word, the most secret 64
of all: thou are greatly beloved by Me, hence I will
speak for thy good.

Center thy mind on Me, be devoted to Me, sacri- 65
fice to Me, revere Me, and thou shalt come to Me.
I promise thee truly, for thou art dear to Me.

Abandoning all (other) duties, come to Me 66
alone for refuge. I shall free thee from all sins: be
not grieved.

This is never to be spoken of by thee to one who 67
is without austerity, nor to one who is without devotion, nor to one who is not obedient, nor to one
who speaks evil of Me.

He who shall declare this supreme secret to My 68
devotees, and display the highest devotion to Me,
shall doubtless come to Me.

There is none among men who does more pleas- 69
ing service to Me than he, nor shall there be anyone dearer to Me than he on earth.

And he who shall study this sacred dialogue of 70
ours, by him I would be worshiped with the sacrifice of wisdom. Such is My thought.

And the man who hears it with faith and without 71
cavil, even he shall be liberated and shall attain to
the radiant world of the righteous.

Has this been heard by thee, O Pārtha, with con- 72
centrated thought? Has thy delusion of ignorance
been destroyed, O Dhananjaya?

Arjuna said:
My delusion is destroyed and I have gained 73
memory (understanding) through Thy grace, O

Acyuta! I stand firm with my doubts dispelled; I shall act by Thy word.

Sanjaya said:
Thus I have heard this marvelous and thrilling   74
dialogue between Vāsudeva and the great-souled
Pārtha.

By the grace of Vyāsa, I have heard this supreme   75
secret, this yoga, from Krishna, the Lord of Yoga,
relating it Himself in person.

O King, remembering again and again this won-   76
derful and holy dialogue between Keshava and
Arjuna, I rejoice again and again.

And remembering again and again that most   77
wondrous form of Hari, great is my astonishment,
O King, and I rejoice again and again.

Wherever there is Krishna, the Lord of Yoga,   78
and Pārtha the archer, there assuredly is prosperity,
victory, happiness and firm righteousness, so I believe.

*

*This is the eighteenth chapter, entitled "The Yoga of
Freedom by Renunciation"* (mokshasannyāsayoga).

Here the *Bhagavadgītā-Upanishad* ends.

Notes

In the following notes only those terms and expressions which have specific philosophical value, together with certain proper names whose meanings are not likely to be clear to the reader, have been selected for explanation. The various readings of the text by the classical commentators (e.g., Shankara, Rāmānuja) are not compared here, nor has attention been drawn, except occasionally, to difficulties that are present in rendering certain non-philosophical passages. These comparisons and problems are exceedingly important for textural criticism but are, we believe, best treated in specialized linguistic studies.

CHAPTER I

1. Dhritarāshtra: the blind King of the Kurus. In the general narrative of the "great epic," the *Mahābhārata,* Dhritarāshtra gave his throne to his nephew Yudhishthira (a brother of Arjuna) instead of to the eldest of his hundred sons, Duryodhana, who was cruel and selfish. Duryodhana conspired nevertheless to gain the kingdom and arranged to have Yudhishthira invited to a series of dice games. Yudhishthira, who had a weakness for gambling, lost badly in the games; in fact, he lost his entire kingdom and, by the stakes of the final game, he (together with his brothers and their common wife Draupadī) was exiled for thirteen years. Dhritarāshtra, who was displeased with this, promised the Pāndavas that after this time and upon the fulfillment of certain conditions they could return to their kingdom and reclaim it. But when the period of exile was over Duryodhana refused to give up his position and power. All attempts at reconciliation between the cousins failed and so both sides appealed to other relatives and friends, who joined one or the other forces. The great battle was then ready to begin.

2. Pāndu: brother of Dhritarāshtra, whose clan is now to engage in the fratricidal war with the Kurus. Pāndu is the father of Yudhishthira, Bhīma, Arjuna, Nakula, and Sahadeva.

3. Sanjaya: the charioteer of Dhritarāshtra, who relates to him the events of the war.

4. *kurukshetra*: Kuru field (located near modern Delhi).

5. Drona: the teacher who taught the art of war to both the Pāndava and the Kuru princes.

6. Drupada: the King of Pāncāla, father-in-law of Arjuna; Dhrishtadyumma is his son.

7. Yuyudhāna: a charioteer; also called Sātyaki.

8. Virāta: King of the Matsyas.

9. Dhrishtaketu: King of the Cedis.

10. Cekitāna: a warrior.

11. Purijit: a warrior.

12. Kuntibhoja: brother of Purijit.

13. Shaibya: King of the Shibis.

14. Yudhāmanyu: a chieftain in the Pāndava army.

15. Uttamaujas: another chieftain in the Pāndava army.

16. Son of Subhadrā: Abhimanya, whose father is Arjuna.

17. Draupadī: wife of the five Pāndava brothers.

18. Bhīshma: an old warrior who brought up both Dhritarāshtra and Pāndu.

19. Karna: Arjuna's half-brother.

20. Kripa: brother-in-law of Drona.

21. Asvatthāman: son of Drona.

22. Vikarna: third of the hundred sons of Dhritarāshtra.

23. Son of Somadatta: Somadatti; father is King of the Bāhikas.

24. *aparyāptam*: insufficient; also has the sense of "unlimited." Professor J. A. B. van Buitenen in an article "A Contribution to the Critical Edition of the Bhagavadgītā," *Journal*

of the *American Oriental Society* (Vol. 85, 1; Jan.–March 1965), has suggested, on the basis of the readings of the *Gītā* by Bhāskara and other commentators, that this verse may best be translated as: "That army, guarded by Bhīma, is not equal to us; on the other hand this army, guarded by Bhīsma, is equal to them." This is a very reasonable rendering, but it doesn't seem to fit too well in the context of the following verse.

CHAPTER II

1. *anāryajushtam* (*an-ārya + jushta*) : unbecoming to an *āryan* or "not acceptable to the noble"; *āryan* (literally, "noble").

2. *prajñāvādān* (*prajñā + vāda*) : words of wisdom; in this context, "tall talk," for Arjuna is not yet learned enough to exhibit real understanding or spiritual insight.

3. *dehin:* embodied soul (also II, 22, 30, 59, etc.).

4. *mātrāsparshās* (*mātrā + sparsha*) : contacts with the objects of the senses or "contacts with material elements."

5. *amritatvāya:* immortality.

6. *asat:* non-being, "the unreal," or "that which is non-existent";
   sat: being, "the real," or "that which is existent."

   These terms come to have a rather precise philosophical meaning in later Vedānta (e.g., in Advaita *sat* is that which is permanent, eternal, and properly applies only to Brahman; *asat* is that which never appears as a datum of experience because of its self-contradictoriness, as "the son of a barren woman") and were used extensively in Upanishadic cosmological speculation. In the *Gītā* the terms seem to be employed only in a general, non-technical sense.

7. *avināshin:* indestructible.

8. *avyaya:* immutable.

9. *nitya:* eternal.

10. *anāshin:* indestructible.

11. *aprameya:* immeasurable, incomprehensible.

12. *antavat:* perishable.

13. Cf. *Katha Upanishad,* I, 2, 19.

14. *aja:* unborn.

15. *shāshvata:* everlasting; constant, eternal.

16. *sharīra:* body.

17. *sarvagata:* all-pervading; omnipresent.

18. *sthānu:* unchanging.

19. *acala:* immovable.

20. *avyakta:* unmanifest.

21. *acintya:* unthinkable.

22. *avikārya:* immutable.

23. *avadhya:* indestructible.

24. *pāpa:* sin or evil in general; primarily that which violates social norms rather than the will of a god.

25. *buddhi:* "intellect," "reason," "faculty of discrimination." Indian philosophy generally distinguishes two aspects of mental life, called *manas* and *buddhi. Manas,* or "sense mind," is the instrument which assimilates and synthesizes sense impressions and brings the self into contact with external objects. It lacks discrimination, though, and thus furnishes the self only with precepts which must be transformed and acted upon by a higher mental function, the *buddhi.* This is the faculty of judgment, that which gives rise to intellectual beliefs and makes understanding possible.

    The *Gītā* also sometimes uses the term *prajñā* to denote "intelligence" or "wisdom" in a somewhat more substantive sense.

26. *samādhi:* concentration. The term also has the meaning of "trance" or "yogic insight," the concentrating of all mental faculties upon a single object.

27. *dvandva:* pairs, suggesting various opposites like pleasure and pain, cold and heat, etc.

28. *niryogakshema* (*nir-yoga* + *kshema*): not caring for the possession of property, more literally, "free from acquisition and possession."

29. *phala:* fruit. This term is employed extensively in the *Gītā* to connote the results or consequences of one's actions; that which is produced by them.

30. *samatva:* serenity or equilibrium, evenness of mind.

31. *buddhiyoga:* discipline of intelligence; means of attaining correct discrimination or intellectual insight; the concentration of the *buddhi.*

32. *karmasu kaushalam:* skill in action; the perfection which results from concentrated activity carried on without being obsessively concerned with the results of the activity. See essay on Karma Yoga.

33. *sthitaprajñasya (sthita + prajña)* : man of steady mind or "one who has firmly established wisdom" or "man of stabilized mentality."

34. *kāma:* desire; sensuous delights. See Introduction for use of the term as one of the "aims of life."

35. *ātman:* self. The *Gītā* uses the term *ātman* extensively, sometimes suggesting by it the "universal Self," "the real Self of man," etc., and perhaps more often suggesting by it the "individual self," the *jīva,* the *purusha.* Although these meanings sometimes shade off into one another in the text, it is usually not too difficult to determine the meaning by the context in which the term appears.

36. *anabhisneha:* not attached, disinclined.

37. *abhinandati:* be pleased or delighted.

38. *dveshti:* upset; dislike, be hostile to.

39. *indriyas:* (the) senses—the usual five with *manas* sometimes taken as the sixth.

40. *vishayas:* objects (or pleasures) of sense.

41. *param:* the Supreme, the highest.

42. *sanga:* attachment.

43. *prasāda:* serenity, calmness of mind.

44. *bhāvanā:* concentration, determination.

45. *nirvāna:* bliss. For early Buddhism, with which the term is usually associated, *nirvāna* was taken in its literal meaning

of "extinguishing the flame of desire," or that state of being which is attained when all desire is extirpated. The *Gītā* uses the term only in a non-technical way to mean simply the bliss or joy that comes with spiritual experience.

CHAPTER III

1. *karmendriyāni* (*karma* + *indriya*): organs of action; or the five "motor organs"—tongue, feet, hands, the ejective and generative organs.

2. *smaran:* dwells; literally, "remembering."

3. *niyata:* allotted or "that work which is prescribed by one's *dharma.*"

4. *yajña:* sacrifice. See essay on Karma Yoga.

5. Prajāpati: Lord of creatures; frequently mentioned in the Rig Veda.

6. *kāmadhuk:* granter of your desire; a mythical cow who satisfies all wishes.

7. *akshara:* the Imperishable. The term was used in earlier Brahmanism as the primal syllable, the indestructible sound which possesses all meaning, and was identified with Brahman, the Absolute.

8. *artha:* interest; purpose, motive.

9. *siddhi:* perfection.

10. *lokasangraham* (*loka* + *san-graha*): maintenance of the world; the term connotes maintaining or guarding the social order rather than ensuring the course of the physical world as such.

11. *pramāna:* standard, measure.

12. *ahankāra:* egoism; technically "I-consciousness" or principle of differentiated self-consciousness in Sānkhya.

13. *tattvavit* (*tattva* + *vid*): he who knows the true essence of, or "one who knows the real nature of"; the term *tattva* also connotes "truth."

14. *gunakarmavibhāgayos* (*guna* + *karma* + *vi-bhāga*): separation (of the soul) from both the *gunas* and action, or division of *gunas* and action.

15. *akritsnavidas (a-kritsna + vid)*: knows only a part, or "not knowing the whole."

16. *adhyātmacetasā (adhi + ātma + cetasā)*: consciousness (fixed) on the supreme Self.

17. *mata:* doctrine; opinion.

18. *shraddha:* faith. The term suggests not so much adhering to a creed as having the disposition to orient one's life around a spiritual teaching.

19. *niyojita (ni + yuj)*: compelled, constrained.

20. *adhishthāna:* basis or seat, foundation, etc.

21. *jñāna:* wisdom; *vijñāna:* understanding. The distinction between these two terms is often drawn in the *Gītā* and, although at times the precise meaning of the terms is impossible to establish, the *Gītā* generally seems to have *jñāna* signify "spiritual wisdom" or "intuitive insight" and *vijñāna* "intellectual understanding," or "worldly knowledge."

CHAPTER IV

1. *yuga:* age or "period of the world." See *infra,* note to VIII, note 6.

2. *tapas:* austerity. The term *tapas* has a long history in Indian literature and is often used in the context of yoga to signify a concentration of energy or "heat." In the *Gītā* the term seems to signify simply "practice," "effort," or "concentration."

3. *cāturvarna (cātur-varna)*: four-caste system. See Introduction on *dharma.*

4. *ashubha:* evil or disagreeable.

5. *yukta* (from *yuj*): harmoniously; literally, "joined," "united," "disciplined."

6. *kāmasankalpavarjitās (kāma + san-kalpa + varjita)*: free from desire (*kāma*) and will (*san-kalpa*).

7. *kilbisha:* "sin," "guilt"—as with *pāpa*, violation of social norms.

8. The second half of this verse is somewhat obscure. It is often interpreted (e.g., by Shankara) to mean the offering of oneself as a "sacrifice."

9. *kalmasha:* sin, guilt. As before.

10. *parisamāpyate* (*pari* + *sam-āp*) : is completed, culminated, terminated.

11. *pavitra:* purifier.

12. *sanshaya:* doubting. A man of a doubting nature (*sanshaya-ātman*) for the *Gītā* is not one who so much questions a teaching or refuses to believe it as one who stubbornly refuses to carry it out in practice. For this reason he is said "to perish."

CHAPTER V

1. *sannyāsa:* renunciation; the giving up of actions prescribed by one's social *dharma* in constrast to performing these actions without attachment to their results (*karma yoga*) .

2. *nityasannyāsī* (*nitya* + *sannyāsin*) : the eternal renouncer; one who always renounces action.

3. *ādhāya* (gerund of *ā* + *dhā*) : having placed (or resigning) his actions in Brahman, or "recognizing" that Brahman, as *prakriti,* alone acts.

4. The "nine gates" refer to the eyes, ears, nostrils, the mouth, the anus and the sex organs.

5. *prabhu:* the sovereign Self, or "the Lord."

6. *vibhu:* the all-pervading Spirit, or "the Lord."

7. *samadarshinah* (*sama* + *darshina*) : look equally or "see the same"; "see with an eye of equality."

8. *brahmayogayuktātmā* (*brahma* + *yoga* + *yukta* + *ātman*) : "his self joined by yoga to Brahman" or "his self disciplined in yoga on Brahman."

9. *moksha:* liberation; release, freedom. See Introduction.

CHAPTER VI

1. *kārana:* means or "the cause."

2. *sarvasankalpasannyāsī* (*sarva* + *san-kalpa* + *sannyāsin*) : renounced all desires or "renouncing all purposes."

3. *yatacittātmā* (*yata* + *citta* + *ātman*) : with mind and self controlled or "restraining his thought and his self."

4. The *Gītā* is describing here some of the essential character-istics of *rāja yoga,* the physical and psychological discipline codified by Patañjali in the *Yoga Sūtra* (2nd century B.C.).

5. *sankalpaprabhavān* (*san-kalpa* + *pra-bhava*) : born of ego-ism; "arising from the will."

6. *brahmabhūtam* (*brahma* + *bhūta*) : become one with Brah-man or "become Brahman."

7. *brahmasansparsham* (*brahma* + *san-sparsha*) : unity with Brahman or "contact with Brahman."

8. *ātmaupamyena* (*ātma* + *aupamya*) : the same for himself or "equally in himself."

9. *sāmya:* equality or "non-difference," "sameness." The state of evenness of mind which follows from a strict controlling of the senses, etc.

10. *shabdabrahman* (*shabda* + *brahman*) : rules of the Veda; the word of Brahman or the injunctions set forth in the Veda.

CHAPTER VII

1. These are among the basic categories or principles of the Sānkhya system which are used to explain the manifested world (or *prakriti* in its evolved state). It is not clear here just how far the *Gītā* is concerned to correlate, rather than incorporate, the principles of Sānkhya with its own more "theistic" principles.

2. *aparā:* lower; *parā:* higher. See Essay II on "Meta-Theology."

3. *jīvabhūtam* (*jīva* + *bhūta*) : life-soul or "indwelling life" or "life-element."

4. *etadyonīni* (*etat-yoni*) : arise from this—probably referring to both the "higher" and "lower" nature of the Divine.

5. *sādhibhūtādhidaivam* (*sa* + *adhi-bhūta* + *adhi-daiva*) : to-gether with (My) material and divine domains or "to-gether with over-being and over-divine." This compound sug-gests again the "higher" and "lower" aspects of the Lord.

CHAPTER VIII

1. *adhyātman* (*adhi* + *ātman*) : supreme Self; the "over-Soul."

2. *svabhāva:* essential nature or "innate nature"; the individual as he is apparently distinguished from the spiritual and material domains.

3. *bhūtabhāvodbhāvakaras* (*bhūta* + *bhāva* + *ud-bhāva* + *kara*) : "that causes beings to exist" or "that causes the birth of states of being" or "brings into existence all beings."

4. *tadbhāvabhāvitas* (*tad-bhāva-bhāvita*) : formed in that state or "made in that condition."

5. *brahmacarya:* chastity.

6. The *Gītā* here presents a form of the general Hindu mythocosmological schema which divides a world period (a *mahā-yuga*) consisting of 4,320,000 years into four ages (*yugas*). The ages are defined in terms of their relative time intervals and the relative degree to which *dharma* or "righteousness" prevails. The four *yugas* are named after various sides of the dice used in gambling.

   Krita, the first of the *yugas,* is the "golden age" in which life is exceedingly virtuous. It lasts for 1,728,000 years, and is named after the side of the die marked with four dots. This is followed by the *tretā yuga,* which exhibits a weakening of virtue, lasts for 1,296,000 years, and is named after the side of the die which has three dots. Then comes the *dvāpara yuga* of 864,000 years in which vice or *adharma* begins to predominate. It is named after the side of the die marked with two dots. The last cycle is the *kali yuga,* the "dark age," which lasts for 432,000 years. During this last cycle, named for the side of the die with only one dot, *adharma* is said to dominate.

   These cycles when rotating a thousand times are said to make for one day of Brahmā or for one Kalpa. Creation occurs and endures during the day of Brahmā, at the end of which time it dissolves for the same period of time, which is one night of Brahmā.

7. Cf. *Chāndogya Upanishad,* IV, 15, 5.

CHAPTER IX

1. *pratyakshāvagamam* (*pratyaksha* + *avagama*) : understood immediately or "known by immediate experience."

2. *sansāra:* ceaseless birth and rebirth—the chain of transmigration which characterizes all ordinary life.

3. *ākāsha:* ether. One of the five material or gross elements in Sānkhya. The term denotes "space" conceived of as fine materiality.

4. *kalpa:* cycle. See note 6 to Chapter VIII.

5. *ekatvena:* as the one or "by the oneness"; *prithaktvena:* as the distinct or "by the manifoldness" or "in many different manifestations"; *bahudhā:* as the many or "in many particular things."

6. Soma: an obscure drink, believed to produce vivid hallucinations, which was used in Vedic ritual.

7. *svargaloka* (*svarga-loka*) : world of heaven, where desires are satisfied but not transcended.

8. *bhoktā:* literally, "the enjoyer," but in this context perhaps rendered best as "the receiver" or "the recipient."

9. *pāpayonayas* (*pāpa* + *yoni*) : literally, "of sinful wombs," but suggestive only of "low origin." For the traditional Hindu attitudes toward women, see *Laws of Manu* (III, 55–60; IX, 2 ff.) .

CHAPTER X

1. *ahinsā:* non-injury or "non-violence."

2. The seven great seers and the four Manus—in Hindu mythology the first manifestation of Brahman in the world, Hiranyagarbha, produced seven seers who were the primal teachers of wisdom and four Manus or rulers of the world who possessed divine powers. Ordinary men are said to be descended from them.

3. *bhāva:* literally, "state," but here probably "feeling" or "conviction."

151

4. *buddiyoga:* yoga of intellect; here as a means by which the supreme Self is attained.

5. Ādityas: a group of twelve gods.

6. Maruts: the wind gods.

7. Kubera: lord of wealth.

8. Yakshas and Rākshasas: various pre-Vedic, Dravidian demi-gods.

9. Skanda: chief of the heavenly armies.

10. Ashvattha: holy fig tree.

11. Gandharvas: divine musicians.

12. Uccaihshravas: the god Indra's horse.

13. Airāvata: Indra's elephant.

14. Kandarpa: the god of love.

15. Nāgas: mythical snakes.

16. Varuna: god of the waters; important in the Rig Veda as the custodian of law (*rita*).

17. Yama: god of death.

18. Vinatā: Vishnu's bird.

19. Rāma: the hero of the *Rāmāyana*.

20. *dvandva:* the dual compound in Sanskrit.

21. Brihatsāman: a portion of hymns dedicated to Indra.

22. Gāyatrī: meter of twenty-four syllables.

23. Mārgashīrsha: the first month of the ancient Hindu calendar; includes parts of the winter months of November and December.

CHAPTER XI

1. *madanugrahāya (mad + anu-graha):* as a favor to me or "out of compassion for me."

2. *kāla:* time; here identified with the supreme Spirit.

3. Vāyu: wind god.

4. Agni: god of fire.

5. Shashānka: the moon.

CHAPTER XII

1. *matparā:* intent on Me or "those who regard Me as the highest."

2. *abhyāsayogena* (*abhi* + *āsa* + *yoga*) : yoga of practice or "constant effort."

3. *aniketa:* homeless or "not having a regular home."

CHAPTER XIII

1. *sharīra:* body or, more generally, "material nature."

2. *kshetra:* field, in a quasi-technical sense.

3. *kshetrajña:* knower of the field or "one who has consciousness of objects."

4. *brahmasūtrapadais* (*brahma-sūtra* + *pada*) : aphorisms about Brahman. The *Gītā* may be referring here to the *Brahma-Sūtra,* the systematic treatment of the Upanishads which tradition attributes to Bādarayāna, but there is little reason to believe that it refers to the text as it has come down to us, for it is not likely that it had been set down in its final form during the time that the *Gītā* was composed.

5. Once again the *Gītā* draws on the basic categories of the Sānkhya system; here, the "gross elements" (*mahābhutas*), the "I-sense" (*ahankāra*), the "intellect" (*buddhi*), the unmanifested (*avyakta*) —or nature in a state of equipoise— the "ten senses"—the five usual senses and the five organs of action. The *manas* and the *tanmatras* or "subtle elements" are not here included.

6. *dosha:* evil or "defect."

7. *tattvajñānārthadarshanam* (*tattva* + *jñāna* + *artha* + *darshana*) : insight into the end of essential knowledge or "vision of the end of knowledge of truth" or "understanding the object of real knowledge."

8. *ābhāsa:* appearance or "semblance."

9. *kāryakaranakartritve*
    hetuh prakritir ucyate/

kārya: acts or effects; *karana:* causes; *kartritva:* agency; *hetu:* causes.

This is a difficult passage and may also be rendered as "*Prakriti,* it is said, is the cause of effects, instrument or agent."

10. *upadrashtri:* witness or supervisor, onlooker.

11. *anumantri:* consenter or permitter.

12. *bhartri:* supporter.

13. *bhoktri:* experiencer or enjoyer.

CHAPTER XIV

1. *jñāna:* wisdom, spiritual knowledge—but in this context perhaps "mere intellectual knowledge."

2. *jaghanyagunavrittisthā (jaghanya + guna +vritti + sthā):* abiding in the lower activities of the modes, or "enveloped in the scope of the lowest *guna.*"

3. *dehasamudbhāvan (deha + sam-ut-bhāva):* whose origin is in the body or "which arise from the body."

CHAPTER XV

1. *jīvabhūtah (jīva + bhūta):* becomes a living soul or "becomes an individual person."

2. *smriti:* memory.

3. *apohana:* argument or "disputation" in general; the term also connotes "loss" or "rejection."

4. *paramātman:* supreme Self.

CHAPTER XVI

1. The *Gītā* seems to be referring to some variety of materialism (*cārvāka; lokāyata*) which might have been current at the time.

2. *shāstra:* scripture; laws or teachings.

CHAPTER XVII

1. *sattvānurūpā* (*sattva* + *anu-rūpa*): in accord with his innate nature or "following the form of the body" or "according to the essential nature of the being."

2. *brahmavādinām* (*brahma* + *vādin*): "knowers of Brahman" —in this context it probably means those who practice the way of ritual or those who expound the meaning of ritual.

CHAPTER XVIII

1. *adhishthāna:* the body or "the seat," "the basis"; *karta:* the agent or "the doer"; *karana:* instrument; *ceshta:* activity or "motion"; *daiva:* destiny, "fate," "the divine."

2. *anahanvādī:* not egotistic; not talking about himself.

3. *dhyānayoga:* yoga of meditation; or, if taken as a *dvandva* compound, "yoga and meditation."

Essays on the
GĪTĀ

An interpreter of the *Bhagavad Gītā* must make certain assumptions about the basic meaning and nature of the text as well as offer valuations and explications of it. Among the many and varied attempts to interpret the *Gītā* one finds, at one extreme, the assumption that the *Gītā* gives voice to a systematic, self-consistent, clearly articulated philosophy. The great classical Indian commentators (Shankara, Rāmānuja, etc.) were driven to adopt this position because of their commitment to *shruti* and *smriti,* to the authority of the "revealed" and "traditional" texts; and they tried to exhibit the systematic unity of the *Gītā* in relation to their own philosophical-religious orientations. In recent years a number of neo-Vedāntic writers, both Indian and Western, have also worked from this assumption, but philosophically they have done so in a somewhat less forceful and less precise manner than the classical writers. In any event, a simple, direct reading of the text suggests to most of us today that this assumption about the *Gītā*'s philosophical intentions is somewhat misplaced, that it is quite impossible to work all of its many strains of thought and values into a complete, systematic unity.

At the other extreme one finds the assumption that

there is very little philosophical consistency in the text because the *Gītā* is essentially a "poem" which appeals to the "emotions": it may display an artistic integrity, but it does not exhibit philosophical unity. One might agree that there "is no system of thought in the *Bhagavad Gītā,* in the sense of a unitary, logically coherent, and exclusive structure of metaphysics" (Edgerton), but it would certainly be a mistake to conclude from this, as apparently some interpreters have, that there are many systems of thought in the *Bhagavad Gītā,* in the sense that it sets forth a multiplicity of logically incoherent structures of metaphysics.

A "middle way" to approach the *Gītā* would seem to be wisest, and would work from the following assumptions:

1. That the *Gītā* is neither a systematic philosophical treatise nor a mere "poem," but that it attempts to integrate many philosophical ideas and religious values into a unified pattern—with mixed results.

2. That many of the apparent inconsistencies in the text can be understood, and even highly valued, if one sees them in the context of a "progressive teaching" function (see Introduction).

3. That some of the attempts at philosophical synthesis in the *Gītā* are tentative or at best incomplete, but that they are not on that account "incoherent."

The task of the interpreter of the *Bhagavad Gītā* would thus be one of examining just what philosophical unity the text does have, where it fails to achieve consistency and why, and what aspects of its thought stand in need of further development.

The following Essays are undertaken in the spirit of this "middle way."

The Nature of Karma Yoga

One who has disciplined his intelligence leaves behind in this world both good and evil deeds. Therefore strive for yoga, for yoga is skill in action.

[II, 50]

This world is in bondage to *karma,* unless *karma* is performed for the sake of sacrifice. For the sake of that, O son of Kuntī, perform thy action free from attachment.

[III, 9]

. . . man attains the Supreme by performing work without attachment.

[III, 19]

The central concern of the *Bhagavad Gītā* is to set forth a way whereby Arjuna may obtain freedom and self-realization through acting in the world. The *Gītā* does vindicate the spiritual value of every discipline, yet for Arjuna, for the man of an active temperament who raises the question of the meaning of "duty" with a highly developed moral consciousness, it offers a very special discipline of action—*karma yoga*. The instruction of *karma yoga* given to Arjuna is, I believe, the central or core teaching of the *Bhagavad Gītā*.

Karma yoga is often treated in Indian (Vedāntic) philosophy as a simple discipline designed for persons of an active disposition and somewhat low intelligence. It is thus to be sharply distinguished from the discipline of devotion, *bhakti yoga,* and especially from the higher, more difficult discipline of knowledge, *jñāna yoga.* My contention, however, is that the *karma yoga* put forward in the *Gītā* is a complex discipline which necessarily involves *bhakti* (devotion) and *jñāna* (knowledge) ; that it involves, in fact, a combined *karma-bhakti yoga* which is preliminary to a combined *karma-jñāna yoga,* with the latter allegedly issuing in a pure *bhakti,* which in turn gives rise to a perfect *jñāna.*

The term *karma,* as we have seen, means "action," "work," "deed," and is used traditionally to mean an action which inevitably produces cértain results or impressions (*sanskāras*) in the actor, and which function as determinants to his future action. *Karma,* in its widest traditional sense, then, means acts performed with the motive of attaining some end or fruit (*phala*) , such acts binding one to future action. It is further assumed that this "law" of action implies a series of rebirths in the actor, with his respective place in the social order dependent upon the moral quality of his acts. *Karma* thus produces bondage to the world.

> This world is in bondage to *karma,* unless *karma* is performed for the sake of sacrifice. . . .

But what, one may ask, does it mean to perform action as a sacrifice? What is being sacrificed? to whom? for what?

The term *yajña*, or "sacrifice," as used by the *Gītā* in the context of *yoga*, does not suggest the giving up of something which is otherwise intrinsically good or desirable, nor does it mean simply ceremonial, ritualistic action (for this is always directed toward the attainment of a "phenomenal" end) ; it means rather the redirecting of one's being away from an involvement with the fruits of one's action to an eternal Spirit which is at once in and beyond the phenomenal world. *Yajña* means the turning away from our lower self (of desires, attachments) for the sake of our higher spiritual self. It means self-surrender for the sake of self-realization. It means acting in the Spirit rather than through the ego; hence the injunction: "Perform thy action free from attachment."

In order to act without attachment, without those egoistic motives for the fruits of action that bind one to the world, one must concentrate one's attention upon the Divine: one must fill one's consciousness with the power of loving devotion. Implicit in the whole teaching scheme of the *Gītā* is the belief that there is no other way to establish non-attachment than through a new attachment to that which is greater, in quality and power, than that to which one was previously attached. One overcomes the narrow clinging to results, the passionate involvement with the consequences of one's action, only when that passion is replaced by one directed to the Divine. *Bhakti* or devotion is thus in no way excluded from *karma yoga,* but is, on the contrary, a necessary condition for it.

In a somewhat narrow, but not infrequent interpretation, *karma yoga* is thought to apply only to those actions which are specifically enjoined by one's duty (*dharma*) to the social order. This narrowing of the sphere of action to which *karma yoga* applies does have some apparent justification, for the *Gītā* argues that one must always work in accord with one's *dharma* and that one should never strive to fulfill another person's *dharma*.

> Better one's own *dharma*, though imperfect, than another's well performed. Better death in (the fulfillment of) one's own law, for another's law is dangerous.
>
> [III, 35]

But the context here is not so much that of marking out a sphere of action to which *karma yoga* applies as it is the urging of Arjuna on to the task at hand, namely the battle. Krishna would have Arjuna sanctify all acts in a spirit of loving concentration upon the Divine.

> Whatever thou doest, whatever thou eatest, whatever thou offerest, whatever thou givest, whatever austerities thou performest, do that, O son of Kuntī, as an offering to Me.
>
> [IX, 27]

Yajña, as applied to all actions, means then a self-surrender to the Divine, not in simple resignation or quietistic withdrawal, but rather in an active state of *nishkāma karma*, action without desire for the fruits. And this is possible only if one is able to recognize the indwellingness of the Divine in the structures of Nature (*prakriti*) and the real nature of human action with respect to these structures. This recognition is the task of a preliminary *jñāna* or knowledge of the world.

This preliminary *jñāna* (or *sānkhya*, as it is often called in the *Gītā*) involves the understanding that all actions of the self are really only the action of Nature acting through one.

All actions are performed by the *gunas* of *prakriti* alone. But he who is deluded by egoism thinks, "I am the doer."

[III, 27]

The *gunas* (*sattva, rajas, tamas*), of which the *Gītā* has so much to say in the concluding chapters, determine one's action. It is not the self who is the real doer, but the whole of one's past experience conjoined with the energies that constitute the natural orders of the world. This teaching of "determinism," which will be analyzed more closely later on, serves many functions in the discipline of action. Somewhat paradoxically, it makes possible just that skill in action which is the final empirical result of *karma yoga*; for it demands that success is possible only when the self unself-consciously co-operates with Nature; that freedom is possible only where there is law and order. As David Hume pointed out in the eighteenth century, the opposite of law is not freedom but chaos. It is only when one functions harmoniously with the inner causal matrix of some action—be it wrestling, cooking, painting, or anything else—that it achieves its natural-spiritual fulfillment. This is the final empirical result of *karma yoga,* but it is not its ultimate meaning for the freedom of man. Something more than perfect empirical action is required, and this leads to the second function that the preliminary *jñāna*—that the self is not the real doer—serves. It is the bringing of the self to the awareness that there is a fundamental distinction between the empirical self and the real Self, that one is not really the self that one ordinarily believes oneself to be; and a full realization of this is precisely the task of *jñāna yoga*.

For Arjuna, *karma yoga* as expressed in its *bhakti* mode as a loving sacrifice, the performing of all acts in the spirit of devotion cannot be the full import of the teaching on the nature and meaning of action—for this *karma-bhakti yoga* can only with the utmost difficulty be reconciled with the duty of a warrior to slay his enemies in battle. It would be ludicrous to kill an enemy on the battlefield, to slay another person with perfection, solely in the spirit of loving devotion to God.

In many places in the *Gītā* it is urged that the wise man, the true yogin, is one who acts with "serenity of mind" or with "tranquillity." He treats all things equally, or, negatively expressed, is indifferent to any value distinctions between them.

> Fixed in yoga, O winner of wealth, perform actions, abandoning attachment and remaining even-minded in success and failure; for serenity of mind is called yoga.
>
> [II, 48]

> Sages look equally on a Brahmin endowed with knowledge and breeding, or on a cow, an elephant, and even a dog and an outcaste.
>
> [V, 18]

> That yogin who is satisfied with wisdom and understanding, who is unchanging and has subdued his senses, to whom a lump of clay, a rock and gold are the same, is said to be disciplined.
>
> [VI, 8]

The true Self of man is thus a state of being which is unaffected by empirical action and is a pure witness to this action. It is a state of unqualified consciousness and joy, of oneness and self-transcendence, without spatial or temporal limitations. When centered in one's Self, one is indifferent to the world. Having found the source and substance of all bliss, all other attractions and distractions are denied. And in this state of being, any action can be performed; for here all value discriminations are swept away in the awareness of the supreme value of the Self. Intensity of devotion must thus be conjoined with the knowledge that the self which thinks, desires, wills, and feels is not exhaustive of oneself; it is only a partial expression of the Self which ideally and really *is*.

> He who knows that it (the soul) is indestructible and eternal, unborn and unchanging, how can that man slay, O Pārtha (Arjuna), or cause another to slay?
>
> [II, 21]

The complete attainment of this self-knowledge, however, which is the goal of a pure *jñāna yoga*, cannot be the final word addressed to Arjuna. For though no act is prohibited, neither is any enjoined.

> As the fire which is kindled makes its fuel into ashes, O Arjuna, so the fire of knowledge makes all actions into ashes.
>
> [IV, 37]

> . . . All action, without exception, is completely terminated in knowledge, O Pārtha.
>
> [IV, 33]

Arjuna must act, however, and in a meaningful way. Arjuna must thus return to *bhakti*, but one which is now fortified by, and derived from, a knowledge of the Self. In the concluding chapter of the *Gītā*, Krishna states:

> Having become Brahman, tranquil in the Self, he neither grieves nor desires. Regarding all beings as equal, he attains supreme devotion to Me.
>
> [XVIII, 54]

The "Me" here is the *purushottama,* the highest Spirit, incarnate as Krishna; a Spirit in whom both the silent Brahman, undifferentiated oneness, and the active *Īshvara,* Being with infinite qualities, are said to be present and reconciled. It is when a higher *bhakti* which follows from *jñāna*—from serenity of mind and insight into the Self—is present that action can be undertaken that is free from attachment to its fruits. For it is through this higher *bhakti,* according to the *Gītā,* that one attains the highest *jñāna* about the nature of the Divine Being and unity with It.

> By devotion he knows Me, what my measure is and what I am essentially; then having known Me essentially, he enters forthwith into Me.
>
> [XVIII, 55]

To sum up: the *karma yoga* which I interpret to be the central teaching of the *Bhagavad Gītā* necessarily involves *bhakti* and *jñāna* in a very special and intimate way. In order to act without attachment to the fruits of action (otherwise, action means a loss of freedom), it is necessary that one perform one's action in the spirit of sacrifice, *yajñā.* This means to perform action with loving attention to the Divine; it means to redirect the empirical self away from its ego-involvement with needs, desires, passions. When this is done, any action can be performed with skill. But freedom, not perfect action as such, is the goal; it is the *motive* of conforming to one's duty in the spirit of non-attachment, not the objective quality of one's act, that is crucial. Simply to kill someone with a skill that is engendered by a loving good-consciousness is clearly inadequate. Hence the necessity to integrate *karma* with *jñāna*—with first a preliminary *jñāna* that shows how Nature acts according to its own necessity, the self never being a genuine doer; then with a deeper *jñāna*, an insight into the nature of the Self, which yields evenness of mind, an equal regard for all things (regarding all things as equally valuable or equally without ultimate value). When acting in this spirit, one can carry out the action required by one's *dharma*. But something more is needed to obtain that complete freedom of spirit which the *Gītā* holds forth as a possibility to man. The *jñāna* of the Advaitin renders all action superfluous; no act is prohibited, but neither is any enjoined. Arjuna, then, must transform this knowledge of the Self into a still higher *bhakti* which has as its object a supreme Person, the *purushottama,* which is the seat, abode, or ground for both Brahman and Īshvara, the personal god. This higher *bhakti,* which makes possible a real diversity-in-unity, culminates in a perfect insight into Reality which brings one into unity with the Divine. And from this unity of man with the Divine, a man is able to fulfill his *dharma.* He acts in the knowledge that all action is essentially the Divine's action. He becomes an instrument of the Divine. He imitates the Divine by acting in the spirit of non-attachment and in so acting his freedom is realized.

II

The Meta-Theological Structure

It is extremely difficult, if not impossible, to set forth with exactitude the metaphysics (or, as we will use the term, "meta-theology") of the *Bhagavad Gītā*. The reason for this is not that there is a paucity of meta-theological data in the text but, on the contrary, that there is such an abundance of it, an abundance which gives rise to a great variety of meta-theological distinctions. A rather coherent scheme nevertheless does appear, and, although it is not without its logical difficulties, it can be outlined in its general form.

The *Gītā*, as pointed out earlier, presupposes the Upanishadic speculation about, and affirmation of, the being and nature of Brahman, the Absolute, yet it upholds a more "theistic" or "personalized" interpretation of reality, and indeed suggests at times that Brahman itself has its ground or abode in a personal divinity.

> My womb is the great Brahman; in that I place the seed, and the birth of all beings comes from that, O Bhārata.
>
> [XIV, 3]

For I am the abode of Brahman, of the immortal and imperishable, of eternal righteousness and of absolute bliss.

[XIV, 27]

And:

There are two spirits in this world, the perishable and the imperishable. The perishable is all beings and the imperishable is called Kūtastha (the unchanging).

But there is another, the highest Spirit (*purushottama*), called the supreme Self, who, as the imperishable Lord, enters into the three worlds and sustains them.

Since I transcend the perishable and am higher even than the imperishable, I am renowned in the world and in the Vedas as the highest Spirit.

[XV, 16–18]

The highest designation of Reality in the *Gītā* is thus not the Brahman of Advaita Vedānta, the non-personal, silent oneness of being, rather it is what the *Gītā* calls the *purushottama* (*purusha-uttama*) —the "highest spirit" or "person." It would be a mistake, however, to read some kind of ultimate dualism into the *Gītā* on the basis of *purushottama* being the highest category. It is not so much that Brahman, the undifferentiated, distinctionless One, is opposed to the *purushottama;* rather, Brahman and Īshvara (the creative-destructive, distinctly personal god) are each identified with It: each is a primary expression of spiritual being. As Arjuna affirms:

Thou art the supreme Brahman, the highest abode, the supreme purifier, the eternal divine spirit, the first of the gods, the unborn, the omnipresent.

[X, 12]

The highest Spirit, then, is at once Brahman and Īshvara, the first of the gods. And It is unknowable.

> Only Thou knowest Thyself by Thyself, O Supreme spirit (*purushottama*), Source of beings, Lord of creatures, God of gods, Lord of the world!
>
> [X, 15]

The distinction between Brahman and *purushottama*, in the sense described, is maintained not only dogmatically but also in terms of the requirements of religious experience. Krishna instructs Arjuna in the nature and difficulty of the Advaitic *jñāna yoga,* the path of pure knowledge to Brahman, and suggests that a yoga of action and devotion centered on *purushottama* manifest as Īshvara is easier.

> The difficulty of those whose minds are fixed on the Unmanifested is much greater; the goal of the Unmanifested is hard for the embodied to attain.
>
> But those who renounce all actions in Me and are intent on Me, who worship Me with complete discipline and meditate on Me,
>
> These, whose thoughts are fixed on Me, I quickly lift up from the ocean of death and rebirth, O Pārtha.
>
> [XII, 5–7]

Īshvara, the creative Lord (symbolized as the god Vishnu who is identified with Krishna), is that presentation of the highest spiritual reality which wields the power of *māyā* and is the ground of both *purusha* and *prakriti*. It is the true dweller in the body of man and it is the ultimate will or law of material nature. It thus manifests itself in a higher (*parā*) and lower (*aparā*) way as "soul," "person," and as "nature," "material being."

In Chapter XIII, the distinction between *purusha* and *prakriti* is cast into a somewhat more epistemological form in terms of the distinction between the "knower of the field" (*kshetrajña*) and the "field" (*kshetra*). And here the Lord, Īshvara, indicates his role as the true knower, as the essential reality of the embodied soul.

> This body, O son of Kuntī, is called the field, and he who knows this is called the knower of the field. . . .
>
> Know Me as the Knower of the field in all fields. . . .
>
> [XIII, 1–2]

The distinction between *purusha* and *prakriti* (with each being an eternal manifestation of the Lord) is further articulated in terms of their respective functions.

> *Prakriti* is said to be the cause of the generation of causes and agents, and *purusha* is said to be the cause of the experience of pleasure and pain.
>
> The *purusha* abiding in *prakriti* experiences the *gunas* born of *prakriti*. . . .
>
> [XIII, 20–21]

Like the Sānkhya system, then, the *Gītā* makes a clear distinction between *purusha* or "soul," "person" and *prakriti* or "material nature"; but unlike the Sānkhya it goes on to overcome the distinction in a higher spiritual synthesis. When knowing the field, the knower does not, as in Sānkhya, obtain an isolation of the soul for its own sake, rather he disentangles himself from the Divine's "lower nature" for the sake of intimacy with the Divine's "higher nature."

The fundamental meta-theological designations in the *Gītā* are the *purushottama,* the supreme spiritual person who is disclosed in Its two primary aspects as the distinctionless Brahman and as Īshvara, the creative-destructive Lord. It further manifests Itself as the individual soul or spirit, *purusha,* and as the principle of Nature or material being, *prakriti,* from which all particular things arise. *Purushottama* is in a sense identical with these manifestations of Itself, and yet is not to be identified with them—that is, It is not exhausted by them. The principle of multiplicity is real. The world is not *māyā* in the Advaitic sense of the term, for everything is taken as an actual self-manifestation of a supreme spiritual Reality. The *Gītā* thus exhibits monistic, theistic, and pantheistic dimensions. The Divine Reality is a state of oneness, It is a transcendent creative power, and It is the essential ground, the indwelling spirit of all that is.

But does this meta-theological scheme present some serious philosophical difficulties? One serious problem that the *Gītā* faces is brought about by its somewhat facile harmonization of Brahman and *purushottama,* the highest Spirit taken as a "personality." By the very definition of Brahman as "oneness" (as that which is "one without a second"), it does not seem either in theory or practice that Brahman can have an "abode" in a still more fundamental or valuable mode of being. Logically, or even experientially, it is not possible to uphold a distinctionless oneness and a more personalized being as Its ground. What could possibly be a "ground" of Brahman when the latter is taken in the first place as the very foundation of all possible being? Classical Advaita Vedānta makes this perfectly clear in its emphasis upon the Upanishadic distinction between *nirguna* Brahman, the attributeless, qualityless Reality, and *saguna* Brahman, the personal divine being with infinite attributes—with the latter being a representation of the former to us in our ignorance (*avidyā*) of Reality. Reality, as *nirguna* Brahman, is non-dual. From the standpoint of *avidyā* or *māyā* one can maintain the idea of there being an actual transformation (*parināma*) of Brahman in the world, but from the standpoint of Reality everything else is necessarily mere appearance (*vivarta*). Advaita Vedānta, in other words, has a theory of incommensurable levels which consistently makes sense of differentiation in the Divine Nature. Lacking such a theory, it seems that the *Gītā* is unable to set forth meaningfully the relations that obtain between the various differentiated orders of the Divine. It suggests that there is no incompatibility between the Divine as being without distinction and the Divine taken as a "personal" being with attributes—but it leaves unanswered the question as to how this is possible.

If the *Gītā* were to assert, as other later theistic forms of Vedānta do, that Brahman as such is qualified by material nature and the soul, and hence is not an undifferentiated reality (e.g., Rāmānuja's *Vishishtādvaita*) or that Brahman is Reality which manifests itself to human beings as a living spirit with whom human experience best fulfills itself by fellowship with, or worship of, this personalized expression of Brahman rather than with Brahman directly, then the *Gītā* would have a reasonable and perhaps even a very strong case to make. One could agree, as indeed the vast majority of Hindus do, that Brahman is the seat of Īshvara (who may manifest Himself as any one of a host of divine beings) but that, because of the actual nature of man, man has a richer, more valuable, and rewarding spiritual life by establishing his religious orientation toward Īshvara rather than toward Brahman in Itself. It could be argued that to attain union with Īshvara is the best that most men can accomplish; and although not the highest form of experience open to man, from any spiritual point of view which affirms Brahman, it would still be a very significant accomplishment.

The Value of
Ceremonial Religion

Where does the *Gītā* stand on the question of the value of "ceremonial religion"—the Vedic cult of sacrifice and ritual which was dominated by the "priestly class"? On the one hand, the *Gītā* marshals several arguments against ceremonial religion and treats it quite sarcastically; on the other hand, it insists that ceremonial religion is both valuable in itself and necessary for spiritual life.

The attack on ceremonial religion takes several forms. It is argued first of all that the correct performance of ritual actions, founded as they are upon the desire for empirical, transitory rewards, only leads to rebirth and not to ultimate freedom *(moksha)*.

The ignorant, O Pārtha, whose selves consist of desire, who are intent (only) on reaching heaven, and who say there is nothing else, rejoice in the letter of the Veda and utter those flowery words which give rise to many ritual performances for the attainment of enjoyment and power, but which result in rebirth as the fruit of these actions.

[II, 42–43]

Ceremonial religion here is clearly not a sufficient condition for *moksha,* and indeed it is not even a necessary condition for it.

Even if a man of very evil conduct worships Me with undivided devotion, he too must be considered righteous, for he has resolved rightly.

[IX, 30]

And for one who has attained freedom, ceremonial religion is utterly superfluous.

As much use as there is for a pond when there is everywhere a flood, so much is there in all the Vedas for a Brahmin who understands.

[II, 46]

When thy intelligence shall cross the tangle of delusion, then thou shalt become indifferent to what shall be heard and to what has been heard (in the Veda).

[II, 52]

But in Chapter XVII we read:

The sacrifice which is not in conformity with the scriptures, in which food is not given, in which hymns are not recited nor fees paid, and which is devoid of faith, they declare to be *tamasic.*

[XVII, 13]

And in Chapter VI:

He who does the action that should be done without concern for its fruits, he is a *sannyāsin,* he is a yogin, and not he who does not light the sacred fires and performs no rites.

[VI, 1]

And in the final chapter:

> Acts of sacrifice, gift and austerity ought not to be
> abandoned, rather they should be performed; for sacri-
> fice, gift and austerity are purifiers of the wise.
>
> [XVIII, 5]

> These actions ought to be performed, abandoning at-
> tachment and fruits, O Pārtha; this is My decided and
> highest judgment.
>
> [XVIII, 6]

But where, then, does the *Gītā* stand? Ceremonial religion leads to rebirth; it is neither a necessary nor
sufficient condition for freedom; it is superfluous for
one who has attained freedom, and yet it is "My decided and highest judgment" that ritual acts ought to
be performed!

The answer to this inconsistency perhaps is to be
found in the various teaching contexts within which the
different positions are taken. The context of the attack
upon ceremonial religion is clear. It is believed that a
one-sided reliance upon ceremonial religion becomes a
formidable obstacle to the attainment of a higher spiritual freedom. The *Gītā* believes that the correct performance of rites and rituals will bring about the desired results (IV, 12; IX, 20–21), and it is precisely
because of their efficacy that they must be set aside. The
Gītā nowhere criticizes ceremonial religion rationalis-
tically as mere superstition and magic; rather it is because it can be effective that it is dangerous in binding
men to the world. When involved in it, men rest content with empirical things and ends and neglect the
ultimate values of life. Vedic ritualistic orthodoxy, in
short, is right in its claims but wrong in its values.

The teaching context for the positive affirmation of

ceremonial religion is not quite so clear; but neither is it entirely opaque. The performance of Arjuna's duty as a *kshatriya*, his *dharma*, would be jeopardized by a complete withdrawal from ceremonial religion, for the Veda which puts forth injunctions about his *dharma* is the same as the one which extols rite and ritual. One cannot throw away the source and retain the offspring when the *raison d'être* of the offspring directly follows from an affirmation of its source. The Veda, in the broad sense of the term used by the *Gītā,* is the source of both the specific ceremonial rites and the dharmic injunctions about duty and obligation.

The final answer given—that one ought to perform the rites but without attachment—actually annuls the whole meaning of the rites which have their grounding in ego-desire, while at the same time it maintains the validity of the Veda as the source of duties and obligations. In short, the *Gītā* qualifies its pointed attack on ceremonial religion by affirming some instrumental value to it, but ironically only when it negates itself. The source of *dharma* thus stands unchallenged; and although some might object that a net of delusion has been cast over Arjuna, he at any rate is prepared to fulfill his *dharma* in the spirit of *karma yoga*—and that is what the *Gītā* is really all about.

IV

Freedom and Determinism

One of the most interesting and difficult problems to be found in Indian philosophy, and especially in the *Bhagavad Gītā,* is the problem of "freedom" and "determinism." To what extent is man "determined" in his empirical experience? What effect does "determinism" have upon his quest for, and attainment of, spiritual experience? And how is "freedom" to be understood in empirical and spiritual terms?

The *Gītā* denies that man has a "free will" over the empirical events or happenings in his life in three interrelated ways. First, according to the *Gītā,* Nature (*prakriti*) is constituted by, and is the source of, the three "strands" or *gunas* which operate according to a strict causal necessity. "Everyone," we are told, "is made to act helplessly by the *gunas* born of *prakriti*" (III, 5). And "There is no thing on earth or in heaven or even among the gods who is free from these three *gunas* born of *prakriti*" (XVIII, 40). The *gunas* are present, in special combinations, in each person, and are the fundamental (involuntary) sources of his action. The individual *qua* individual is never the real doer, but is only an expression of an indifferent energetic Nature which compels him to act. In short, as is one's "energy system," which one can never originate but only accept, so is the kind and quality of one's action.

Second, the *Gītā* accepts, as one of its basic philosophical assumptions, the law of *karma*—that every action (whether physical or mental) carries along with it determinants for future action. Each man has his *dharma*, his order of obligations and duties, his proper place in society which results from his past actions. And man must work within the restricted domain of his karmic-based *dharma*.

> That which thou wishest not to do, through delusion, O son of Kuntī, that thou shalt do helplessly, bound by thine own action [*karma*] born of thy nature.
>
> [XVIII, 60]

The principles of *karma* and *dharma* do, however, presuppose some element of non-deterministic choice; they do not so much prescribe the exact or specific decision that one will make in a given situation as the general disposition or tendency to act in a certain way. *Dharma*, especially, carries along with it the idea of moral obligation, the demand that certain actions be performed, and this clearly implies some degree of free choice on the part of the actor. No moral quality can be attached to the doer of an involuntary act or to the act itself. *Karma* and *dharma* do nevertheless prevent a man from initiating an act which does not follow from, or is independent of, the causal matrix of *prakriti* and the laws of his own psychic nature. Further, the slight degree of "free will" which is implicitly affirmed by the

principles of *karma* and *dharma* is definitely overruled
by the third meaning of "determinism" in the *Gītā*,
which is that everything in Nature and man is ultimately ruled over by the Divine and, in a very real
sense of the word, is "predestined" by Him.

In Chapter XI, where Arjuna is vouchsafed the stu-
pendous vision of God, the Lord reveals Himself as
having already decided the future course of events.

> Time am I, the world destroyer. . . . Even without
> thee, all the warriors arrayed in the opposing armies shall
> cease to be.

> Therefore stand up and win fame. . . . By Me they
> have already been slain. Be thou the mere instru-
> ment. . . .
>
> [XI, 32–33]

And finally in the last chapter Arjuna is told:

> The Lord abides in the hearts of all beings, . . . caus-
> ing all beings to revolve by His power (*māyā*) , as if they
> were mounted on a machine.
>
> [XVIII, 61]

Man, then, is bound by the *gunas* of *prakriti;* he is
bound by his own past action (*karma*) as this crystal-
lizes into a law (*dharma*) of his own nature; and he is
bound by the will of God who ordains the ultimate
course of all events. The *Gītā* thus instructs us in several ways (which are not brought together into a single
synthesis) that we are not the free-willing beings we
ordinarily take ourselves to be. It would agree with
Spinoza that we think we are free because we are aware
of our desires, but we are actually in bondage because
we are ignorant of the causes of these desires. And in

further agreement with Spinoza, the *Gītā* understands bondage to consist in a lack of self-determination, in being subject to external conditions, in being conditioned by "passion," in not having "adequate ideas"; it is only then that Nature, one's own past experience, and the Lord become blindly compelling.

The state of bondage does not exhaust the potentialities of our human status. It is indeed the case that we are in bondage insofar as we are empirical, phenomenal beings centered in our egos, but for the *Gītā* we are something more than empirical, phenomenal beings: man is a spiritual being who can attain to a state of freedom which annuls all bondage.

In the somewhat negative sense of freedom *from,* we can—as is clearly implied in the following verse—attain to a freedom from the play of the *gunas* functioning within us.

> When the embodied soul transcends these three *gunas,* whose origin is in the body, it is freed from birth, death, old age and pain, and attains immortality.
>
> [XIV, 20]

One can attain freedom with respect to the "strands" of one's material nature through a knowledge (*jñāna*) of Nature and through a love (*bhakti*) of God. When a man ceases to act out of ego-dominated needs because he sees and understands the structure of Nature and his essential relations to the Divine, he is no longer bound by this Nature. The act of understanding and love (*amor Dei intellectualis*) brings an independence from what would otherwise be tyrannical. One's empirical actions must still have causal antecedents, for otherwise there would be chaos. It is a philosophical commonplace that one could not determine oneself in a situation where no causal relations were present. Rather than detracting from the quality of freedom, then, this causal matrix, properly understood, makes possible just that self-conditioning which is the essence of freedom.

Man can also, according to the *Gītā,* overcome the law of *karma* operative in him through a yoga grounded in *jñāna.*

> Actions do not bind him who has renounced actions in yoga, who has cast away doubt by knowledge, who possesses himself. . . .
>
> [IV, 41]

When we cease to be attached to the fruits of our action, we are untouched by them. What effect can something have upon us when we are indifferent to it? The man who is self-possessed is not possessed by something else. By understanding the nature of action, of the actor, and his field of action, he is released from bondage to action. If centered in the Spirit, nothing that he does can affect him.

Lastly, and in a somewhat paradoxical way, a man attains freedom from the omnipotent will of God by co-operating with it. According to the *Gītā,* he who is in perfect obedience to the Spirit is free. He who is in perfect accord with the true nature of being is self-determined: his actions arise from the fullness of his essential nature. Freedom is possible and meaningful only within the structure of Divine Nature. One is free when one no longer has an ego-centered empirical will of one's own. To be an "instrument" of the Divine means to be rid of everything that narrows one's nature and one's field of action; it means to participate in, and to reflect, the utter freedom of the Divine.

Freedom, for the *Gītā*, is clearly incommensurate with bondage. Freedom is not the antithesis of "determinism," for it is not on the same level of being as that to which determinism applies. Freedom is different in kind from bondage; it is *sui generis*. It is ultimately the quality of the man who realizes himself as a spiritual being. Recognizing his ultimate unity with the Divine, he acts joyfully, in perfect accord with Its will.

How, though, is this freedom to be obtained? The answer, or rather answers, given by the *Gītā* are set forth in terms of the various yogas which it prescribes. One crucial point, however, which needs to be made here is that the *Gītā* recognizes that there cannot be any mechanical or guaranteed path to freedom. A yoga can only be a *necessary* but never a *sufficient* condition for freedom. If freedom could be obtained as a definite result of a series of specific physical, emotional, or mental acts, then it would causally be a part of that series and would lose thereby its *sui generis* nature. Yoga prepares one for freedom, but no yoga can ensure its attainment. It is thus that the *Gītā* introduces the idea of "grace" (*prasāda*).

The concept of "grace" is not, however, treated very fully in the *Gītā*. This is somewhat unfortunate as, in a curious sort of way, it seems to be the link between "determinism" and "freedom" as these are understood in the poem. However, at least two senses of "grace" are acknowledged. The first is the familiar notion of divine intervention—the free-willing entry of the eternal into the temporal for the purpose of aiding someone in their spiritual quest. This divine intervention, or "giveness," on the part of the Divine takes place for the *Gītā* when man prepares himself adequately to receive it.

> But to those who worship Me, thinking of no other, to those who are constant in perseverance, I bring acquisition and possession of their goal.
>
> [IX, 22]

When man seeks the Divine, the Divine may meet him; and if he is to attain freedom, the Divine must meet him; He must make steady his path.

> Go to Him alone for shelter with all thy being. . . . By His grace, thou shalt obtain supreme peace and the eternal abode.
>
> [XVIII, 62]

> But whatever form a devotee with faith wishes to worship, I make steady that faith of his.
>
> [VII, 21]

The second sense of "grace" is somewhat more difficult to grasp and does not appear in the *Gītā* quite as explicitly as does the first. But it is the only one which is compatible with the affirmation of Reality as transcendent and as without attribute. "Grace" here becomes fundamentally a category of our ignorance. It involves an acknowledgment of our ignorance about how freedom can be obtained by a man caught up in the world. Logically expressed, to affirm "grace" is to acknowledge the inability of the rational mind to know what the sufficient conditions are for freedom. If it is the case that no yoga can ensure the desired end of freedom, then there is something unintelligible in principle about how it is possible to bridge the gap between the soul embodied in *prakriti* and its true spiritual abode. The affirmation of "grace" is thus an acknowledgment of the "mystery of being." It points to that which is unintelligible—to that which is "wonderful" and "marvelous." It points, in short, to the indeterminate or undeterminable quality which makes possible the transition from the level of determinate being to the level of free being.

To sum up: The position of the *Bhagavad Gītā* on the question of "freedom" and "determinism" is complex. It suggests that man is bound, as an empirical being, to his own psycho-physical nature (as expressed in the doctrine of the *gunas*), that he is bound to his own past experience (*karma*) as this becomes formative of his nature (*dharma*), and that he is bound by the omnipotent will of the Divine. But man's nature and his range of action are not essentially restricted to the empirical domain. Through a self-transcendence of ego and desire, through an act of love and knowledge, man may overcome all of the sources of that which determines him. The resultant self-determination or "freedom" is not, then, the mere opposite of "bondage," as it is not on the same level of being as "bondage"; it is *sui generis*, unique in quality. To attain this freedom requires a complete self-surrender and a disciplining of oneself through yoga. The attainment of freedom, however, cannot be understood entirely in causal terms. By its very uniqueness it defies explanation in terms of that which it transcends; hence the necessity to appeal to a doctrine of "grace." Apart from suggesting a "movement" of the Spirit toward man, as man makes a movement toward It, the notion of "grace" involves the noetic recognition of just this inability of man to explain his essential freedom. The assertion of "grace" becomes the acknowledgment that freedom itself cannot be determined.

Conclusion

The *Bhagavad Gītā* is a magnificent philosophical-religious poem. Without self-conscious artistry, it succeeds in awakening one to profound dimensions of oneself and the world. By presenting its teachings in a vivid existential setting, it gives the reader a sense of vital participation in a spiritual quest. Its teachings are not just theory (or *theoria*); they have an urgency about them, a compelling demand for fulfillment and realization in action.

Philosophically, the *Gītā* does not, as pointed out before, offer any highly original world view or organization of human experience. It stands to Brahmanic and indigenous popular tradition in much the same way that Dante's *Divine Comedy* stands to the work of Thomas Aquinas—with the difference that the *Gītā* did not have as complete a system from which to draw. The *Bhagavad Gītā* is synthetic; occasionally it lacks apparent consistency, and many complex themes are not fully developed in it. Nevertheless, its call for self-knowledge, and its clarification of what this means, has enduring significance. Man, it insists, is not a mere "thing"; rather, he is a person who realizes himself only in his deepest relations to the structure and power of Being. The special philosophical-religious contribution of the *Gītā* is its teaching that this realization can be obtained in many ways, and that there is a path to freedom for the man of action in the world. The *Gītā* sees clearly the possibilities in every spiritual discipline, and encourages men of every temperament to find and fulfill the discipline appropriate to them. This is indeed a teaching that has meaning and value for all times and places.

Bibliography

As indicated in the Introduction, the *Bhagavad Gītā* has been
translated many times into English and other Western languages.
It has been translated quite literally (e.g., by Franklin Edgerton)
and it has been translated quite freely (e.g., by Edwin Arnold and
by Christopher Isherwood and Swami Prabhavananda), and in
almost every possible way between these extremes. Each translation of the *Gītā* tends to contribute something to our understanding of it; and no single translation is ever likely to be satisfying
to everyone, either on philosophical or literary grounds. The student, therefore, is strongly advised to consult several translations
in his study of the text. Among the numerous English translations
of the text, the student is advised to select from the following:

Lionel David Barnett. *Bhagavad-gītā*. London: J. M. Dent & Sons,
1926.
Annie Besant and Bhagavad Das, *The Bhagavad-Gītā*. Adyar,
Madras: Theosophical Publishing House, 1940.
Franklin Edgerton. *Bhagavad Gītā*. Cambridge: Harvard Univer-
sity Press, Harvard Oriental Series, Vols. 38 and 39, 1944, 1952.
W. Douglas P. Hill. *The Bhagavadgītā*. London: Oxford Univer-
sity Press, 1928.
Swami Nikhilananda. *The Bhagavad Gītā*. New York: Rama-
krishna-Vivekananda Center, 1944.
K. T. Telang. *The Bhagavad Gita*. Oxford: Sacred Books of the
East, Vol. 8, 2nd edition, 1918.

Many commentaries have been written on the *Bhagavad Gītā*
in recent years by Indian scholars. The following works differ
rather widely in their interpretations of the text but are of special
interest in illustrating the vital role that the *Gītā* still plays in
Indian culture.

Sri Aurobindo. *Essays on the Gita*. Calcutta: Arya Publishing
House, 1950.

S. Radhakrishnan. *The Bhagavadgītā* (Essays and commentary accompanying his translation). London: George Allen & Unwin Ltd., 1948, 1960.

B. G. Tilak. *The Gītā-rahasya,* translated by B. S. Sukthanker. Bombay: Bombay Vaibhav Press, 1935.

About the Author

Eliot Deutsch was formerly Professor of Philosophy and Chairman of the Department of Philosophy in the School of Humanities and Social Sciences, Rensselaer Polytechnic Institute, Troy, New York, and is now Professor of Philosophy at the University of Hawaii and Editor of the journal *Philosophy East and West*. He was graduated from the University of Wisconsin and received his Ph.D. from Columbia University.